SAM MAC

Accidental Weatherman

hachette
AUSTRALIA

Unless otherwise credited, all photos are from the author's collection.

Published in Australia and New Zealand in 2021
by Hachette Australia
(an imprint of Hachette Australia Pty Limited)
Level 17, 207 Kent Street, Sydney NSW 2000
www.hachette.com.au

10 9 8 7 6 5 4 3 2 1

 A catalogue record for this
book is available from the
National Library of Australia

ISBN: 978 0 7336 4597 6 (paperback)

Cover design by Christabella Designs
Cover photograph courtesy of Are Media Syndication
Text design by Kirby Jones
Typeset in Sabon Lt Std by Kirby Jones
Printed and bound in Australia by McPherson's Printing Group

 The paper this book is printed on is certified against the Forest Stewardship Council® Standards. McPherson's Printing Group holds FSC® chain of custody certification SA-COC-005379. FSC® promotes environmentally responsible, socially beneficial and economically viable management of the world's forests.

Contents

1

3.47 a.m.

Gale force winds, torrential rain, mass power blackouts. Sydney is being battered by its worst November storm in forty-four years.

Australia's top rating breakfast TV show, *Sunrise*, shifts to 'rolling coverage'. That means the breaking news story is considered significant enough to dominate the show. This storm is a major weather event. The perfect time, you would think, for the weatherman to shine. The perfect time, you would think, for the weatherman to impart his in-depth meteorological knowledge to the nation. The perfect time, you would think, for the weatherman to do what weathermen do best: talk about the weather.

So where is the *Sunrise* weatherman as all of this unfolds live on air? He's on the sunny Gold Coast in an ill-fitting

Hawaiian shirt interviewing a talking cockatoo named Gandalf. I am deadly serious.

That's me, Sam Mac, the *Sunrise* weatherman. Sure, most weathermen would consider it a professional insult to be asked *not* to report on a major weather event, but not me – I know that by avoiding detailed weather chat, I can create more room in my segments to do what I do best: tap dancing, baby discos, knitting, riding camels, bungee jumping, massaging strangers, eating the world's hottest chilli, life drawing and even some Bollywood dancing. And I think all of that happened in the one week. Welcome to my life.

You might be wondering what on earth those activities have to do with the weather. And the answer is ... absolutely nothing! The average length of one of my live crosses is around three minutes. Thirty seconds of that is weather related. Which means that this weatherman spends 80 per cent of his air time talking about topics other than the weather. Wonderful news for fans of tap dancing.

On multiple occasions I've even completely forgotten to throw to the weather forecast. That's the entire premise of my segment! I've had a big laugh, or completed a stunt, then casually told the studio team I'd be back with more later in the show. Awkwardly, *Sunrise* hosts David Koch (a.k.a. Kochie) and Samantha Armytage have had to respond with, 'Ahh, Sam, what about the weather?'

People often ask me how I became a weatherman. The answer truly is by accident.

I was working as a waitress in a cocktail bar … Okay, that's a lie. Just checking you're paying attention.

I was working as a roving reporter for *The Project* on Channel Ten. They were the first big show to take a chance on me. It was an extremely fun, smart and supportive team. I was relishing my air time. The problem was, my air time was too sporadic. Despite being on contract, I would occasionally go a full week without a single appearance on the show. So I was effectively being paid to do nothing. And I thought that only happened to TV executives!

(I'm fully aware that joke may jeopardise my future career prospects. Ahh well, thug lyfe.)

Around this time, my great friend Stefan Mitchell was the executive producer for *Weekend Sunrise* on the Seven Network. One afternoon he called to see if I'd be interested in doing a few live crosses from the opening of a new space-themed cat cafe called Catmosphere.

This is arguably the most on-brand brief I've ever received. Cats and puns, yes please.

Technically, *The Project* could've said no. But, as mentioned above, they're good people, and I genuinely felt they had my best interests at heart. I could, however, feel a tinge of reluctance as they officially approved my appearance on Seven. It was like agreeing to an open relationship. I was with Network Ten, my lover, but I had permission to simultaneously be with Network Seven, my mistress. And I was getting paid by both. So, I guess it was less like an open relationship and more like I was a cheap rent boy with two masters. That metaphor ended up far messier than it started. My apologies.

My segments at Catmosphere were a lot of fun and the feedback from Seven was very positive. Stefan told me that Craig McPherson, Director of News and Public Affairs, had instructed him to get me on the show more often. Craig will probably read this book so I want to go on the record to point out that he is *not* one of the executives I was referring to in the joke above. In fact, Craig's been one of my biggest supporters and is ultimately the man who got me over to the network. (I also realise that disclaimer has completely undone my thug lyfe claim.)

So, after only a handful of fill-in spots, I was offered one of the biggest jobs in television, the role of *Sunrise* weather presenter. Throughout the negotiation period, I kept expecting a weather or basic meteorology quiz to be sprung upon me. I even googled a glossary of weather terms just in case. I presumed, as a bare minimum, I'd be sent to a TAFE-style meteorology short course. But it never happened. And so, with absolutely no planning, research or qualifications, I'd just accidentally become a weatherman.

The most common question I am asked about my job is, 'What time do you have to get up in the morning?' The answer is that it varies from day to day, depending on how far I have to travel to the filming location. On an average day, the first of my three alarms goes off at 3.47 a.m. It's always the harshest alarm. But I take great satisfaction in showing it who's boss and going straight back to sleep. The second (or preliminary) alarm goes off at 3.57. This one isn't quite as abrasive, but it brings with it a lingering sadness. I know that with the preliminary alarm, the dream is (literally) almost over. The final non-negotiable alarm sounds at 4.07 a.m. This is the alarm that makes me reassess all of the life decisions that have led me to this point. I often sit on the edge of the bed while the alarm is ringing, and I imagine a different life. Why couldn't I have been a weatherman on a *Tonight* show?

I set three alarms because I prefer the gradual wake-up over the band-aid single-alarm wake-up. I thoroughly enjoy the two moments I get to disobey the alarm, even though the alarm always wins in the end. On the iPhone, there's an option to attach a little note to each alarm. Next to the final alarm, my note says – and I'm not making this up – 'Do it for Kochie'. And that's all the inspiration I need to face the day.

The second most common question I get asked is, 'How many frequent flyer points do you have?' Please don't hate me, but I'm a platinum member with both of Australia's major airlines. I know their lounges so well you could blindfold me at the entrance and I'd still be able to safely find my way to the pancake machine. I started this job in 2016 and in the five years since I've averaged 120 flights a year. In 2018 I caught 137 flights, a personal record. Zero of those were business class. I really need to get Kochie to give me some negotiation tips.

In researching for this book (yes, I actually did some – you're welcs) even I was astonished to learn that as of December 2020 I'd hosted a staggering 7600 segments on *Sunrise*. Including three good ones. I'm joking. There were at least ten.

That equates to approximately 380 hours, or 22 800 minutes of live TV. Even I'm sick of my own face after learning that.

While we're on statistics, I can tell you that those flights have enabled me to visit more than eight hundred Australian towns. As the weatherman I've travelled more than 1.5 million kilometres. I know the airport check-in experience very, very well. So much so that I barely even remember doing it. It's muscle memory. I just put my headphones on with some tunes or a podcast and glide through.

There are only two moments that snap me out of that almost meditative state. The first is when I get patted down at security. I actually look forward to it – it's often the only physical contact I get from another human being for that week. And, yes, it probably *is* unnecessary for me to ask them if they'd like to pat me down again 'just to be safe', but I'm only giving them the option, okay?

The other moment that snaps me out of airport chill mode is seeing the price of sandwiches. My goodness – fourteen dollars for a grim-looking egg and mayo sandwich in a plastic container? I'd rather eat a service station hotdog. And that's a big call, that's opening yourself up to all manner of questionable 'meat'.

We also travel internationally and I've been lucky enough to host the segment from ten different countries. My top five are Japan, Canada, USA, South Africa and the Cook Islands. Picturesque lakes, secluded woodside cabins, private pools, three-hatted restaurants, stunning gondola rides and hot springs in the snow. I've found myself in some of the world's most romantic situations, in some of the world's most romantic locations. The only problem is that I'm completely alone. Or, even worse, with my producer, Sean Flynn, a.k.a. The Human Emoji. I mean, I love Sean, and you're going to learn a lot about him in this book, but some experiences are more enjoyable with a partner, not with an anorexic George Costanza.

Finally, the third most common question I am asked is, 'Where did you study meteorology?' My response to this is uproarious laughter. That question is generally a sure-fire giveaway that the person asking it has never watched the show.

In my first year I used to worry about being exposed, or publicly shamed for living a lie. I had recurring nightmares that an FBI-style organisation called the FBM (Federal Bureau of Meteorologists) was going to track me down, take me off air mid-segment, and ban me from ever discussing the weather again.

But as time passed by, I discovered that my segment was ultimately about two things: people and places. As long as I could entertain and make meaningful connections with the people of Australia, most viewers would ignore the fact that I was a fraudulent forecaster.

And one thing I never expected was how much this job, and the people it enabled me to meet, would transform my life.

2

People

Being welcomed into your lounge room every morning is an absolute privilege. It's something I'll never take for granted. We're so spoilt for entertainment options these days, so when I meet someone who watches our show, I make a point of saying thank you.

As humans, we're often at our most vulnerable first thing in the morning. We've just woken up, and we're fragile. That's why breakfast TV has a unique opportunity to form an extremely powerful bond with the audience. There's an element of trust involved. Familiar faces or voices can be very reassuring. Everybody wants to start their day with a level of comfort, something that's going to make them feel good. That could be a reliable journalist delivering the news, a commentator who inspires robust political discussions, or even a silly weatherman who just makes you smile. The fact that I can start off a stranger's day with a laugh or a smile is one of the most rewarding parts of my job. Second only to the free Cabcharges.

I hosted a lot of radio and TV shows before I started on *Sunrise*. I'd occasionally get recognised out and about by strangers, but it was generally with a hint of confusion or hesitation. Some people would know who I was straightaway, but the vast majority would either think I was a guy who once dated their sister (deny, deny, deny!) or a guy they used to play C Grade cricket with (I would've been A Grade, obvs) or even the guy from the chocolate adverts (do a Google image search for Lindt Master Chocolatier).

All of that changed when I started on *Sunrise*. Almost instantly, people seemed to know who I was with a new degree of certainty. I really noticed it at the airport. Security staff would suddenly address me by name and ask how the cats were. I don't think that's standard protocol.

Thankfully these interactions with strangers were all positive, but being newly recognisable was certainly a little unnerving. I could feel people looking at me or talking about me more than I was used to. I had to quickly adjust and be at ease with it. I mean, I'm hardly a Kardashian, I'm a TV weatherman, but it transformed my little world.

I must confess, I wasn't a *Sunrise* viewer before I got the job. Back then, if I was out of my bed before 9 a.m. I must've wet it. I'm a night owl. But as I started to meet our viewers, I realised I had dramatically underestimated the show's reach and popularity.

Sunrise viewers have an incredible amount of passion for the show, and its hosts. They know intimate details about every member of the team, and they're fiercely loyal. Every day, no matter where I am in Australia, people rush up to me. 'Tell Kochie I'm a Power member!' 'Tell Sam I've got a labrador too, just like Banjo.' 'Tell Beretts I met him at the Melbourne Cup in 2008.' 'Tell Nat I've got a bunion.' 'Can you give Eddy this "Molly" blanket I knitted for her new bub?'

I absolutely love it. It's a compliment of the highest order. And although it's not possible for me to pass on all the comments, I definitely give it my best shot.

(Side note: after reading this, some of my mates will finally understand why they occasionally see me rugged up on the couch in a 'Molly' blanket. Sorry, Eddy.)

My role isn't really about weather (thank goodness). It's about people. I travel the country meeting people from all walks of life. I hear their stories, and I help to share them with the nation. Our average stay in most towns is only about eighteen hours. Arrive early evening. Bed by 8 p.m.

Up at 4 a.m. Do the show. Have breakfast. Head back to the airport for a flight by midday. On to the next town. And repeat. We don't have long to build a rapport, and the lights and camera can make for a very unnatural setting. But, in my experience, if you follow your gut, look people in the eye, and have an open mind, it's quite incredible the connections you can make very quickly.

It doesn't matter whether you're in a preschool or a retirement village, there's a story to tell. And with the added power of social media, I've been lucky enough to enjoy some truly magical connections. Here are a few that have really stayed with me.

In early 2019, one of my great mates, Liam Stapleton, hit me up for a favour. Now, some of you will be familiar with Liam. He used to host the Triple J Breakfast Show (Ben and Liam) and these days can be heard on Nova Adelaide. He's an extremely gifted young man, but he's also very genuine, and I'm proud to call him a pal.

The favour he wanted was for me to make a little video for a close family friend, a man named Chris Grigg. Liam explained, 'Chris is in his early fifties and he was recently diagnosed with motor neurone disease. I know you get requests like this all the time, but he's such an amazing person and this will really lift his spirits.'

Liam continued, 'He's told my mum how much enjoyment he gets out of your segments, and how much that means to him during such a shitty time. He legitimately watches *Sunrise* to see you.'

Obviously I was blown away by such a compliment. I told Liam it would be my pleasure to do a video for Chris, but I'd like to take it one step further and give him a personalised shout-out live on *Sunrise*.

A few days later I shared his story on air: 'The Big Freeze is coming up, raising funds and awareness for MND. And I'd like to take this opportunity to give a shout-out to Chris Grigg, he's a friend of a friend. Chris is in his early fifties, he was a very successful footy player, and these days he runs a gym, very fit, very active guy. All of a sudden, last year, he starts to encounter some health problems. Difficulties with chewing, a dramatic loss of strength in his arms and he's diagnosed with motor neurone disease.'

At this point I put on the 'Fight MND' beanie and said, 'Currently, there's no cure for MND, and we don't know how fast or slow it will affect his body. So I'm wearing this beanie for Chris Grigg today. We're right behind you, mate. We know that you've taken this like a champion, and you've even been lobbying and working behind the scenes to improve assistance and awareness for people with MND in South Australia. You raised an extraordinary forty thousand dollars with the Athelstone Football Club. All of this while going through a battle of your own. You're incredible! I'm also wearing this today to show support to anyone else watching with MND, and their families.'

It was quite an emotional moment. I felt an extra layer of connection because Liam is a close mate of mine and I knew how much Chris meant to Liam's family.

Unbeknown to me, Chris's family decided not to tell Chris he was going to be mentioned on the show. And they secretly filmed him when the segment went to air. They sent me the video later that day.

Chris was on the couch, in his tracksuit, watching *Sunrise* like he does every day. All of a sudden, I mentioned his name and his photo appeared on the TV. His jaw dropped. Thankfully he wasn't live on the air because, as his eyes nearly popped out of his head, he mumbled, 'What the f**k?' Apologies for the language, but totally understandable.

As I shared his story with Australia he was clearly in shock, glancing between the TV and his wife, Samantha, who he could now see was filming him with her iPhone. There was a point in the video where Chris really broke down. It was the part where he saw photos of how he looked before MND, and how he looked now. It was like two different people.

As I watched the video back, I broke down in tears myself. Even though we'd never met, I felt like I knew Chris. I've met people just like Chris at sporting clubs over the years. He's a father, a great guy, and he doesn't deserve this.

When I look at how MND has affected Chris, it really upsets me. It's so cruel, so unfair. At fifty-three, he was fit and healthy, and now he struggles to lift the quilt over himself in bed at night. Not long after his diagnosis, Chris married his partner of seven years, Samantha, in a surprise wedding. That tells you a lot about his character. He really is living for every day and making the most of every opportunity. But he's well aware of the reality of MND. 'It's terminal, I will die,' he told me when we first spoke. 'The average time from diagnosis, they say, is twenty-seven months.' That breaks my heart.

A year into their marriage, Chris had lost all of the strength in his hands and arms and he had to sell the gym. Samantha has taken on the role of carer, helping him shower, eat and clean his teeth. But, much like Chris, she has a wonderfully positive attitude. 'We're trying to live the life we would've lived over the next twenty years, but we're just trying to cram it all in … a few holidays, spend time with the kids and friends,' she said.

Chris and I started chatting regularly and struck up a bit of an Instagram friendship. I love seeing the photos he posts with his kids and Samantha. I also love getting his little updates, on the good days and the bad days. I'm so impressed by the way he's tackling this head-on. He's constantly lobbying and working behind the scenes for better conditions for people with MND. He's also determined to ensure that when his final months do come, he has the option to live them out in comfort at his home surrounded by his wife, his kids, and loved ones. As much as I hope that's many, many years away, I fully support Chris on that mission.

When I returned to Adelaide in October 2020, I suggested to Liam that we invite Chris for a beer so I could finally meet him. Chris had told me many times over messages that he was going to shout me a beer one day. It was only right that I took up the offer. I got such a thrill when he walked into The Archer Hotel in North Adelaide that night. I gave him a big hug and we sat down to spend a few hours chatting and laughing like a couple of old mates. I must be honest, his physical state and his ability to communicate had deteriorated more rapidly than I'd expected, compared to the videos I'd seen. But his spirit was high. And his wit was razor sharp. He was dropping hilarious zingers about Kochie, Port Power and even my lack of weather knowledge. I could, however, sense his frustration at his speech not keeping up with his brain. At one point he apologised to me. 'I'm really sorry if you can't understand all of what I'm saying,' he said. Of course, it was completely unnecessary, but I wanted to keep things light so I responded, 'Mate, I'll be the one apologising to you for my speech if I have a few more beers.' I found out after the fact that Chris almost didn't come that night because he was self-conscious about his speech. Well, I'm so grateful he did, because once a champion, always a champion. And after meeting Chris, I'm adding MND to the list of causes I'll be using my platform to promote and support. But next time it's my shout, mate.

•

In my five years on the show, I've visited over one hundred schools. Kids bring such enthusiasm and unpredictability to life, which often makes for great TV. There's something dangerous about sticking a microphone in front of a kid's face and genuinely not knowing what they're going to say. That works for me – I prefer my crosses to be slightly dangerous. And a little tip for fellow TV presenters: don't just chat to the students put forward by the school. They're often Student Representative Council (SRC) members and will perform like scripted robots. Go out of your way to find the naughty kids. They bring the gold. (No offence to SRC reps – I was one. It's true, I peaked in Year 7.)

Occasionally we meet a student who well and truly steals the show. That's exactly what happened in September 2019 at Rozelle Public School in Sydney. I interviewed ten-year-old Arran Keith. When he was just six months old Arran was diagnosed with cerebral palsy quadriplegia, affecting all four of his limbs. But what struck me immediately was that Arran's all about what he can do, not what he can't. He may be young, but he's already doing enormous things in his chosen sport of race running, an innovative sport for people with a physical disability. Race runners use a running bike, a three-wheeled frame with a saddle, body support and, most notably, no pedals. It's dynamic, and very impressive. Arran was the first Australian athlete to compete in race running in Europe. He even participated in 'Little Warriors' at the Invictus Games and he's conquered the eighteen-kilometre summit of Mount Kosciuszko. All of that by the age of ten!

Arran is a cheeky, highly intelligent young lad who is wise beyond his years. 'The doctors said I would never walk, but now I walk on my own with no one behind me,' he told me. 'Cerebral palsy is not necessarily a disability, I think I have more ability. I want to be a Paralympian or a politician one day.'

In our conversation, live on air, Arran revealed that his hero is Australian sporting great Kurt Fearnley. I'd need an entire chapter to list Kurt's achievements, but he's most famous for multiple gold medals at the Paralympic Games, and for 'crawling' the Kokoda Track. A true legend.

Arran told me that Kurt was a big inspiration to him and that he was currently reading his book. This sparked an idea in my mind. Wouldn't it be great to help Arran meet his idol? So in the next cross I prepped Arran to talk directly to the camera as if it were Kurt Fearnley. I teed up some emotive music (we went with 'Wind Beneath my Wings') and Arran addressed the camera: 'Good morning, Kurt, my name is Arran Keith, I'm a race runner from Sydney, you're my favourite athlete, I'd really love to meet you one day, please don't let Sam and me down.'

The team lost it. Arran's cheeky little ultimatum at the end was a wonderful conclusion to a great segment. Now I was invested in making this meeting a reality. So were our viewers. People were writing to me on social media asking if Kurt had responded, other people were claiming to know Kurt and promising to pass it on. Everybody was on Arran's side. Kurt didn't stand a chance.

I sent a direct message to Kurt on Instagram. He replied within an hour. He told me he'd love to touch base with Arran and asked for his parents' phone number. Yes!

Later that day I received a video from Arran's parents. It showed a very excited Arran in his front yard telling the neighbours (and anyone who'd listen) that he'd just got off the phone from Kurt Fearnley, and he was going to get to meet him soon! Such a beautiful video. I could feel Arran's joy.

Moments like this truly make me happy. It's so fulfilling, to play a part in creating something special for a deserving young boy. I'd also like to pay tribute to Kurt Fearnley – he's the real deal, and the Australian public don't even see half of what he does for youngsters like Arran and their families. I'll leave the final word of this story to Arran's dad, Richard, who got in contact with me a few months after we'd met. He sent me a beautiful photo of Arran and Kurt, and this message that I treasure:

> Hi Sam, I'm Arran Keith's dad and I'd like to say a heartfelt thank you for what you have done for this young man, you made his dream possible. We are currently at the Wheelchair NSW junior camp at Narrabeen (Kurt invited us). Arran is trying loads of brilliant disability sports ... Kurt is a total gent and I think you have changed my family's life ... honestly.

(Courtesy Richard Keith)

•

Another extremely special connection I formed came about after I replied to a direct message on Instagram. I put a lot of time and effort into reading and replying to every single person who writes to me on social media. It's both exhausting and rewarding. It's almost a full-time job, but it matters to me, and occasionally I'll stumble across a diamond in the rough. Like this one.

I received a direct message from a woman named Zandalee. She told me that her mum, Sandra, was about to have a double mastectomy. Messages like this always stop me in my tracks. Zandalee went on, 'I don't really watch TV so I don't know much about you. But my mum talks about you all the time. She tells me funny things you've said or places you've visited and she gets very excited when you "like" her comments. But the reason I'm writing to you is, I'm currently in London studying, I'm so far away on a very scary day in my mum's life, and I want her to know I'm thinking of her.' Zandalee then asked if I could make a little video wishing her mum the best of luck for the surgery.

What an honour it was to be asked, and during such a delicate, private time. I must've tried about twenty-five takes on this video. It was so important to me that I got it right. This is what I said to Sandra in the video:

'Hi Sandra, Sam Mac here. I just wanted to let you know that I'm thinking of you today. I'm sending love and positive vibes ahead of your surgery. Your family got in touch with me because they love you very much, and they care about you deeply. I'd like to leave some final thoughts to one of the great philosophers of our time ...'

And then I broke into a rendition of Christina Aguilera's 'Fighter'.

'You are that fighter, Sandra.'

Much like the Chris Grigg shout-out, Sandra's family secretly filmed her watching the video message. They sent it to me later in the day. There she was, in her wheelchair, minutes away from going into surgery. She pressed play and almost immediately broke down in tears. She gently leaned into the arms of her husband. Sobbing. At the end of the video she said, 'What a beautiful man. Thank you. He spreads love everywhere.' That hit me for six. The fact that I can provide just a tiny piece of comfort or joy during such a traumatic experience is something that truly fills my soul.

No words will be able to do justice in describing how much that moment meant to me. I played a small part in taking Sandra's mind off what she was about to go through but, more importantly, I helped her feel close to, and loved by, her daughter Zandalee who was on the other side of the world. As much as I love making people laugh, it's memories like this that I find the most satisfying. I'm fast becoming the low-budget Oprah.

One of my favourite moments in the video happened as I was quoting the lyrics to 'Fighter' – Sandra clenched her fist and started mouthing the words with me. We were totally in synch. And then, for a brief moment, she smiled. Glorious. It totally vindicated my decision to go with that Christina Aguilera song and not 'Dirrty'.

Sandra and I chat often. She's an incredibly strong, creative, driven woman. Breast cancer is the least interesting thing about her. And she is not letting it define her. As I write this book, Sandra tells me that her health is good and there

(Courtesy Sandra Conte)

are no signs of cancer at the moment. I watch with pride as she continues to achieve wonderful things in the arts world. Sandra is extremely passionate about encouraging women to trust their instincts if they feel something isn't right with their health. I'd like to end this chapter with her beautiful and important words:

> Women, speak up.
> Even if you're made to feel small.
> Whatever you do …
> Listen to the voice inside of you …
> Remain vigilant, diligent,
> uprise, don't compromise,
> you know your body well,
> my scars have that story to tell.

Thank you, Sandra. This is why you're so loved.

3

Coco

There's an old saying that goes, 'You don't choose an animal, an animal chooses you', and I thoroughly believe that's the case with my girl Coco. Even though we found each other in a roundabout way, it truly was meant to be.

I have no doubt whatsoever that many of you only bought this book because of Coco. She's not just a cat anymore. She's a celebrity cat. An icon, even.

Coco has modelled on the covers of magazines, she's amassed tens of thousands of Instagram followers, she's fronted campaigns with brands such as Fancy Feast and, probably saddest of all, she was my date on the Logies red carpet. We'll get to all of that soon enough, but first, the beginnings of a superstar.

I was living in Perth with my ex-girlfriend Patrice. (She was my current girlfriend at the time. Living with an ex-girlfriend would not be fun. For anybody. It actually sounds like a cruel torture technique that could be used to extract information from a hostage. Forget waterboarding, just chuck someone in a room with their ex. They'll cave. Very quickly. Sorry, I digress.)

Patrice is a very passionate animal lover and animal rights advocate. Her knowledge, tenacity and empathy in this area are some of the greatest gifts she ever gave me. Her move from Sydney to live with me in Perth had been a bumpy one. She was missing her friends and family. She didn't like her new job. And, most devastatingly of all, she had to come to terms with the fact that most cafes in Perth close at 1.30 p.m. Inhumane. You want a late lunch? Absolutely not, you psychopath.

Things went from bad to worse for Patrice when her beloved cat of fifteen years, Princess Audrey, went missing. She must've somehow jumped over the balcony when we weren't looking.

We tried everything to find her. We tapped the cat food tin. We knocked on doors. We put up posters. We even hired a pet investigator (yes, it's legitimately a thing just like Ace Ventura, only less charismatic and more expensive). and because I was hosting a radio show at the time, I made a point of describing Princess Audrey every day in case someone had spotted her.

Princess Audrey was a grey cat but the most distinctive thing about her was that she only had three legs. Imagine my excitement one morning when a listener called to say they'd spotted a three-legged cat in the Leederville area (only a suburb over from us). Devastatingly, this cat was black. Who would've thought? Another three-legged cat hobbling around our suburbs. False alarm.

A month passed, and still no sign of Princess Audrey. I was about to fly to Adelaide for the weekend and I remembered Patrice had been talking about a one-eyed cat at the RSPCA where she was a volunteer. His name was Pirate (obviously) and he was up for adoption. I decided to leave the money out and a note saying that if Patrice felt ready then I'd love to give Pirate his forever home. In no way was Pirate intended as a replacement for Princess Audrey, but he deserved a happy life of his own.

Patrice agreed and excitedly headed to the RSPCA with the cat carrier in hand, ready to bring Pirate home. Plot twist: the RSPCA don't keep animals on hold for you, and by the time Patrice arrived someone had already adopted Pirate. She had missed him by half an hour. Patrice was understandably upset. She had her heart set on Pirate. But she decided to walk through the cat adoption centre just in case another cat caught her eye.

She spent a few hours pacing up and down, searching for the right cat. Adopting an animal is a life-changing decision.

One of Patrice's greatest qualities is that she has a heart of gold, and she'll often rescue animals that most people would give up on. When we lived together, she regularly 'found' pigeons that were 'injured' on her walk home from work. At one stage we were nursing two pigeons back to health as well as fostering two kittens in our one-bedroom apartment. The landlord would've had kittens if he'd known. Two of them.

In all seriousness, Patrice is the kind of person who will gladly take something on when no one else will. It's an extremely admirable quality. And it probably explains why she was with me.

It was almost closing time when the RSPCA staff member invited Patrice to have a look at a special 'behind closed doors' area. This area was not technically accessible to the public, and it only housed a handful of cats. These were the cats considered most at risk, or most unlikely to be rehomed. I get emotional as I tell this story, because this was where we found Coco.

Coco had been rescued from a large, empty property, where she had been completely abandoned and left to starve.

She was dangerously malnourished and was essentially a lethargic little ball of skin and bones. The staff told Patrice that if someone hadn't found her within a week, she may not have made it. She was emaciated.

Patrice knew instantly that this was our cat. The staff member warned her that Coco only had a couple of teeth remaining due to severe gingivitis and she would require special biscuits and a closely monitored diet. The woman said that Coco might need to return for veterinary check-ups in the coming months and that some of her medication would be a little pricey. If you know Patrice, you'll know that just made Coco even more desirable. This was an animal that needed a second chance, an animal that needed to be loved.

The staff member must've known she could trust Patrice. True animal lovers connect with other animal lovers in an instant. It's often unspoken. The lady placed Coco on Patrice's shoulder and she sat there, completely still, with a gentle purr. Patrice then handed over the best 175 dollars we'd ever spent and it was time for Coco to begin her new life.

I was more of a dog person growing up. I mean, I liked cats too, but I felt more of a bond with dogs. Particularly a rottweiler I had named Giggs. A gentle giant and an absolute sook. I also had a cat as a youngster. We got him from the Sunday markets for fifty cents and I named him

Tigger. Two weeks later, as I was playing with him, the poor little guy broke his leg. So the fifty-cent cat cost Mum and Dad three hundred dollars in vet fees. My parents remind me of this story a minimum of four times a year.

I was about to fly home from Adelaide when I received a text from Patrice: 'We missed out on Pirate by half an hour! Someone else adopted him! But don't worry, I found the perfect cat. You can see her when you get home.'

I excitedly asked for a photo, but Patrice said she wanted it to be a surprise. She later revealed that there was more of a strategic reason she didn't want to send a photo: she was worried Coco looked too girly and I wouldn't like her.

I have such a clear recollection of the very first moment I laid eyes on Coco. I can see it like it's on an HD cinematic video loop. It's genuinely that clear in my mind. A very precious memory.

I opened the door and there she was. A tiny white fluffball sitting on the couch like she already owned the place. She had a squishy little face and enormous green eyes that shot daggers at me for daring to interrupt her evening. Her look was completed with a slight snarl due to her lack of teeth. Imagine the iconic Elvis Presley lip snarl. But minus the sex appeal. And minus the teeth. And on a cat. I was in love.

I'd never seen a cat like Coco in my life. I know now that she's a Burmilla, a cross between a Chinchilla and a

Burmese. But at the time I just thought she looked like a little alien. My initial reaction was to burst out laughing. Uncontrollable laughter. Guffaws, even. I don't really know what it was, but she just made me laugh. Patrice later told me that she'd never seen my face light up with joy so much as it did in that moment. That's probably another indicator of why our relationship didn't go the distance.

Now, I've been calling her Coco, but up until this stage she didn't have a name. I decided on Coco because it's the nickname of one of my all-time favourite comedians, Conan O'Brien. Patrice seemed surprisingly happy with my name selection. I later found out that, yet again, it was strategic. She approved the name because (a) she thought if I got to pick the name I would bond quicker with the cat and (b) most people would think she was named after Coco Chanel anyway. I only learnt all of that when I spoke to Patrice as research for this book.

The first month with Coco was certainly never dull. She's such an expressive cat. Very vocal and highly irreverent. She also needs to be physically close to humans at all times. Considering what she's been through, it may be a form of separation anxiety. Poor thing. She's more like a dog than a cat. And within a few days she was sleeping on my neck while I was in bed. So it's safe to say she settled in quickly. And by 'settled in' I obviously mean 'was running the house'.

It wasn't all smooth sailing. Coco has a dangerous ability to be simultaneously naughty and stubborn.

I was doing breakfast radio at the time so my alarm was set for 4.07 a.m. Every second of sleep was precious. That didn't stop Coco from deciding that 2 a.m. would be her playtime. Night after night I was woken up by her running laps of the apartment, meowing incessantly and, most annoying of all, hitting table tennis balls against the wall. *Bang, bang, bang.* It was nonstop. At that time of the morning she was a devil cat.

Coco's first taste of fame was in 2011. I was doing a live cross from Perth for Channel Ten's *The Project* and I had an interview with the artist formerly known as the Bondi Vet, Dr Chris Brown. These days Chris is one of my best mates, but in 2011 we'd only just met. The segment was supposed to promote an event Chris was in town for, but I cheekily took Coco along and used our air time to get a free veterinary check-up. Chris played along beautifully and declared Coco a happy, healthy cat.

The piece ended with me showing him Coco's snarl and diagnosing her with a very rare condition known as RBF. Chris was unfamiliar with the term. I informed him he should've studied a little harder at vet school because he should know that Coco suffers from severe Resting Bitch Face.

From there I started to feature Coco in my 'hit' YouTube series 'Lights, Camera, Maction!' Often it would involve me enthusiastically serenading her while she wore a costume and looked extremely unimpressed. Simple, but effective. People started to ask for more of her in my videos. Which I think was code for less of me. This was an early insight into where our eventual hierarchy and popularity were heading.

Time for another plot twist. Almost two months after Princess Audrey had disappeared we received a call from the local vet saying someone had found her. Unbelievable. She'd been attacked by a dog and had obviously been living on very little food for the past eight weeks. The poor thing was in a bad way. Patrice was beside herself. Thankfully, Princess Audrey made it through. She was a tough old thing.

When Princess Audrey returned home there was a slight problem. A fluffy, white problem. Coco. Princess Audrey was not the most sociable feline (she was savage and would rip your face off if provoked). Coco, on the other hand, was playful, inquisitive and full of kitten-like energy.

Despite her traumatic sojourn, Princess Audrey came home swinging. And Coco was in the firing line. Princess Audrey was swiping more than a newly single 22-year-old chick on Tinder after a bottle of prosecco.

The problem was, they both thought it was their house. Princess Audrey had lived there before Coco arrived. And Coco had arrived before Princess Audrey had returned from her adventure. It was beginning to look like Coco might need to be rescued for a second time.

But, thankfully, after a few warning swipes (that definitely made contact) Coco understood that if she stayed well away from Princess Audrey, her life would be much safer. Essentially Coco was learning social distancing about a decade before everybody else.

At the end of 2011 I quit my breakfast radio job in Perth, and Patrice and I moved back to Sydney so I could chase my TV dreams. In Sydney I became an ambassador for Sydney Dogs and Cats Home. It is a relatively small shelter in the suburbs of Sydney doing big things in the field of animal rescue. I loved everything about it. They had a phenomenal team of volunteers, a strict no-kill policy, an open door to any animal in need, and an outstanding in-house vet. Their slogan said it all: 'Rescued is my favourite breed'.

I started by promoting Sydney Dogs and Cats Home on TV and radio. I also made little pieces of content to help rehome particular animals and shared them on my social media. I then became the official emcee for their annual black-tie fundraising gala dinner. It was extremely rewarding, and even though they didn't explicitly say it,

Sydney Dogs and Cats Home had a no dickheads policy. Just great people who loved animals. The joy of seeing a previously abandoned animal run into the arms of its new forever owner is truly magical.

I crowned myself a 'Sambassador' – a nickname that is yet to catch on almost a decade later.

One Saturday morning in 2012 Patrice called me in tears.

'I'm at Sydney Dogs and Cats Home,' she said, 'and there's a blind kitten that desperately needs a foster. Can we please take her? Just for a week?'

Now I don't claim to be the perfect boyfriend, but even I know that when your girlfriend is in tears you immediately do or say whatever is required to stop those tears. So I agreed to look after a blind kitten for a week.

The split second I hung up the phone, I knew that 'a week' meant 'forever'. I knew that I was now going to be living in a one-bedroom apartment with my girlfriend and three cats. A few more cats and we could almost register as a charity ourselves.

Patrice named the blind kitten Cleocatra. I feel like this was another strategic move by her as she knows I love a pun. The name was, however, a little girly for me, so I instantly shortened it to the much manlier name she's known by today, Catra.

So imagine our tiny Paddington abode. I have a blind cat, a three-legged cat, and a cat missing most of its teeth. Between the three of them, we almost had a complete cat. This was not the Sydney life I had imagined.

But once you bond with an animal, it's a bond for life. So this was our little crew. Slowly but surely Princess Audrey, Coco and Catra managed to tolerate each other. My furry family brought my friends much joy; I was an easy target. My mate Wil Anderson accurately pointed out that I was 'one cat away from being an *A Current Affair* story'.

Sadly, in 2013, Patrice and I broke up. From my perspective, it ended slowly. We didn't have the spark we once had. We both still cared deeply for one another, and respected each other, but we weren't on the same timeline. Our relationship wasn't as fun as it used to be. But she will always be a part of who I am and, sadly for her, I will always be a part of who she is.

This put us in quite the predicament. We had three cats to divide between two people. There was never going to be a nasty custody (catsody) battle; we agreed that we just had to do what was right for the cats. Patrice was always going to take Princess Audrey. And I was always going to take Coco. Even Patrice would admit that Coco and I were meant to be. We'd formed an unlikely, yet extremely close bond. Plus she was starring in my YouTube videos.

So that left beautiful Catra. I presumed that Patrice would take her as she was the one who found her at Sydney Dogs and Cats Home and was desperate to give her a loving home. Much to my surprise, Patrice suggested I take Catra because Catra got along better with Coco than she did with Princess Audrey. That wasn't necessarily a major achievement, as Catra got along better with the vacuum cleaner than she did with Princess Audrey. But before I even had time to respond, it was settled, and I was launching my new bachelor life as a man in his thirties with two cats. Hello, ladies.

After Patrice and I broke up, I was very lonely. I wasn't looking for another relationship, and I wasn't ready for one. I'm sure some people will read this and think I'm a freak, but the cats really got me through that period. It's hard to describe, but just having their presence in the house brought a warmth with it. The simple routine of seeing them every day when I got home, feeding them and patting them, gave me a much-needed blanket of comfort and consistency. It's ultimately companionship.

This was a pivotal point in my life. I was beginning to get a reputation as the stereotypical 'crazy cat lady'. You know, the person who dies alone surrounded by a collection of cats that ultimately eat their flesh. I had a big decision to make: either pull back a little on the whole cat thing or double down and be an unapologetically loud-and-proud cat man. You can probably already guess which path I took. And as they say in the classics, #NoRegrets.

It was 2016 when Coco's celebrity status really started to skyrocket. I was regularly showing photos of her to the nation on *Sunrise*. Even Kochie would start some segments by asking, 'How are Coco and Ketchup?' (Five years on the show and he still thinks Catra's name is Ketchup.) On my social media, it was becoming evident that my most popular posts all contained Coco. My housemate (cat-sitter slash unpaid social media assistant) Jasmine Petty noticed this and suggested we give Coco the honour of her very own Instagram page. And so, @lifeofmisscoco was born.

I've been so fortunate to have two dear friends as housemates (cat-sitters slash unpaid social media assistants) while I've been gallivanting around the nation and beyond with *Sunrise*. Without Jasmine Petty and Ally Mansell, I really don't know how it would've been possible. I'd do anything for those women; they became my surrogate family.

It wasn't just that they looked after the cats – they looked after me. And they truly cared. One time, when I was really under the pump with my travel schedule, Jasmine did my washing. She handled my dirty underwear without being asked. If it was the other way around, I'd probably be the subject of a police investigation. And Ally, well, she has one of the biggest hearts you'll ever find in a human being. When I was going through a devastating relationship break-up, Ally checked in on me multiple times every day, and the way that she guided me through that period meant more to me than she'll ever know. I cried when she moved out. Partly because I knew I was going to miss her, but also because I was so elated to know that my blocks of chocolate were finally safe (I knew it was you stealing the chocolate the whole time, Ally!).

Coco's Instagram grew at a rapid rate (i.e. faster than mine). Jasmine and I would workshop photos and ideas together, and the more we posted, the more followers Coco gained. The most enjoyable part of the process was writing the captions from Coco's perspective. Due to her aforementioned RBF (Resting Bitch Face) her character and tone came very easily. Miss Coco was an entitled, narcissistic model, desperate for compliments and attention to hide her obvious deep insecurities. So, essentially, she was like most influencers on Instagram.

They say being selected for Victoria's Secret can elevate you from 'model' to 'supermodel'. Coco had a similar momentous elevation on 15 October 2018 when she was announced as the first Australian cover-cat of *Pussweek* magazine. First of all, I'm deadly serious. It's a highly regarded glossy magazine written by cats, for cats. And, yes, it's honestly called *Pussweek*. Definitely a title you need to be careful with when googling, and no, it does not look good on your credit card statement.

I somehow convinced the *Sunrise* producers to let me broadcast from the launch of Coco's edition of *Pussweek*. Bexy McFly, the author/editor/creator of *Pussweek*, agreed to hide the cover from Coco and me until we revealed it live on air.

We turned the launch into quite the shindig, with decorations and thirty invited guests. The big moment happened live on air just after 8 a.m. Coco arrived in a small child's remote-controlled luxury vehicle. Picture Coco in her rose-coloured sunglasses relaxed and sitting perfectly in a white mini convertible BMW. Marvellous. We had the J-Lo song 'Jenny from the Block' playing as Coco pulled up, because she used to have a little and now she has a lot.

The live cross was mayhem. The brakes slammed a little hard and Coco nearly fell out of her seat. But, ever the supermodel, she took it in her stride, looking fabulous and suitably unimpressed the entire time.

Jasmine picked Coco up and Coco's claw got stuck on Jasmine's blouse, so we were dangerously close to a Janet Jackson Super Bowl moment.

I asked Jasmine and Patrice to stand next to the easel and do the honours of revealing Coco's front cover. I thought it would be a nice touch to have them involved as they'd been such an integral part of Coco's story.

'Five, four, three, two, one!' The crowd cheered and the *Sunrise* hosts in the studio were howling with laughter at the absurdity of what was unfolding before their eyes. And there she was. Coco and her trademark RBF looking resplendent on the cover of *Pussweek* magazine's Christmas edition. The caption read 'Meowy Catmas, Mother Fluffers!' and underneath the stunning picture was the blurb for her lead story: 'A rogue piece of sticky tape was stuck to my bottom, Miss Coco's horrific gift-wrapping ordeal.'

Coco's magazine debut was a roaring success. But it didn't happen without an almost instant backlash. From the very beginning of Coco's Instagram account there's been a question that we haven't been able to shake. That question kept growing and growing until it became its own mini movement. And Coco's appearance on the cover of a magazine only heightened this movement. I'm talking, of course, about the #WheresCatra movement. That's right. I have been repeatedly accused of playing 'favourite child' to Coco over Catra.

They say every book needs a little controversy to ensure it grabs a few headlines. Well, I get a feeling this is mine. I'm slightly nervous to finally address this topic, but I think it has to be done. So here goes. I, Sam McMillan, have been accused on multiple occasions of hiding Catra from the limelight because she's plus-sized and blind. There, I said it. I've even had to delete comments from followers suggesting I'm in some way ashamed of her. Ouch! It's simply not true.

Catra is a social recluse. While Coco is the Kardashian of the cat world, Catra is the Sia. She has no interest in the limelight. She doesn't like being handled, she doesn't like sitting still for photos, and she certainly doesn't like dressing up in a Christmas tutu or cat sunglasses from Japan. All I'm doing is respecting her privacy. She has the sweetest nature, but she's terrified of new noises or new people. Everything has to be on her terms. I love her dearly and she's just as special to me as Coco is. But, I have to be honest, she's just not as photogenic. And she doesn't have the supermodel star power that Coco brings. And that, my friends, is the quote the tabloids will use. It's okay, it's not like she'll be able to read it (she's blind).

As I held that copy of *Pussweek* magazine and looked at the picture of my girl Coco on the front, I felt like a proud dad.

Her journey from rags to riches makes me smile. But there's also a method in my madness. All of the silly props, the wacky photos, the TV segments, the magazines, the wild adventures, they have a purpose. That purpose is to entertain but, more importantly, to promote rescue animals. The work I'm most proud of in my career has been in the space of mental health and animal rescue. Every animal deserves a second chance. And I truly believe that they can sense when you've saved them, and they repay you times a million.

For every copy of *Pussweek* sold, fifty cents went straight to Sydney Dogs and Cats Home. In every interview I did, I promoted the 'adopt don't shop' message. Even within my own friendship group there was still a perception that rescue animals were in some way damaged goods. It couldn't be further from the truth. Walk through any rescue facility and you'll be blown away by how many little gems are waiting there, ready to become the best decision of your life.

My legendary pal Rachel Corbett happened to be watching the live cross where I unveiled Coco's cover of *Pussweek*. She texted me what has to be one of the most accurate descriptions of what I do: 'Sam Mac weather reports: 99% Sam living out his dreams, 1% meteorology'. Well played, Corbes.

It still blows my mind to know that my cats make so many people smile. No matter where I am in Australia with this job, I can walk into a park in Orange or a luxury hotel on Hamilton Island and invariably someone will stop me and say, 'How's Coco?' And it's genuine interest. They want a detailed update. It always puts a smile on my face.

More recently I was at the Pink Flamingo cabaret show on the Gold Coast. I was in the bathroom and heard someone say, 'Oi, Sammy Mac!' I turned around to see one of the most intimidating-looking blokes I've ever laid eyes on. This guy was an absolute unit. Picture Dwayne 'The Rock' Johnson. Shaved head, covered in tatts, totally ripped. I had no idea why he was calling my name.

I quickly finished what I was doing and said, 'Hey, mate, how are you?' He then proceeded to sing the chorus of 'Half Man, Half Cat' – the song I recorded with The Wiggles (you'll read about that later) – complete with choreography. I started pissing myself (this time metaphorically) and he went on to tell me it was his favourite song before asking, 'How are Coco and Catra, buddy?'

See! Catra *is* famous!

For a number of years now I've accepted that some of my social media followers only follow me for the Coco content. If a few weeks have passed without any Coco photos, I'll start to get direct messages asking for her. It's quite phenomenal the bond people seem to have with her.

In 2020 things escalated to another level. I received a call from my manager, Melissa Harvey. She told me there'd been some interest for a client campaign. I asked Mel who the client was, and what they wanted me to do.

'Well, the client is Fancy Feast, and they're actually interested in Coco,' she said.

I'd created a monster.

Mel went on to say, 'I've been in management for many years, but I've never negotiated a deal for a cat.'

Weirdly, that made me proud.

So, a few months later, I was on set as Coco's plus one doing a professional photo shoot with five different looks. Coco and I had a formal look. A nerdy look. A holiday look. A casual look. And a bedtime look. Between each theme Coco was ushered into a bedroom with unlimited chicken Fancy Feast (her favourite) and a selection of toys and blankets. Unbelievable.

For that week at least, Coco was the primary income earner for our household. About bloody time. It's been a ten-year investment, a slow burn, but she's finally contributing!

Coco will hate me for revealing this as it could affect her future modelling opportunities, but she's a senior cat now. We don't know her exact age, but she's at least thirteen. That plays on my mind quite often. One of my biggest fears is that one day I'll have to say goodbye to her. Even imagining that day is traumatic. I often try to change the subject and block it out. But it's a reality, and the hardest part of loving a pet.

I've never experienced a bond with an animal like the bond I have with Coco. I know this probably sounds pathetic, but I feel a higher level of connection to her and she's everything I ever wanted in an animal. She understands me and I understand her.

Whenever I've faced challenges in my life over the past decade or so, she's been the constant. Whether it's missing my family or even the breakdown of a relationship, Coco's always been there. Right by my side. Giving me something else to focus on, making me smile and, my favourite, sleeping on my back. I never trained her to sleep on my back, I never asked her to sleep on my back. It just became her thing. And now it's probably the feeling I look forward to most in the world.

When I lie down after a big, stressful day, I rarely have to wait more than thirty seconds until I hear her footsteps coming up the stairs. Then she'll jump onto my back, settle into a comfy spot, and start purring. It's hard to describe how much that simple gesture settles me. But when Coco's sitting on my back, everything is right in the world.

I really could devote an entire book to Coco (she's going to be livid when she realises she only got one chapter) and maybe one day I will. There's just so much more to her story. But don't stress – there's still more Coco goodness sprinkled throughout this book. We'll learn about a Coco tattoo, and the outrageous mission to make her the first cat ever to attend the Logies red carpet.

This chapter ended up being far more sentimental than I'd intended. But as I always say, if you're speaking from the heart, and speaking your truth, then it's the right thing to do. As I write this section, it's currently been five weeks since I've seen Coco and Catra. The longest work trip I've ever been on. The longest period I've ever spent away from them. Thankfully my former housemate, the incomparable Ally Mansell, has treated them like queens and taken them into her house (ha ha, you thought you'd got rid of us, Ally).

Every day away really does remind me how much they mean to me. I miss them meowing when it's their dinner time. I miss Catra bumping into the walls (I do have my suspicions her 'blindness' is a bit of an act, but at least she commits), I miss seeing their faces as I walk in the door after work, and, of course, I miss Coco sleeping on my back.

Next time you're thinking of welcoming a new addition to your family, please, consider a rescue animal. Whether you want a big dog, a little dog, a kitten, a senior cat, almost anything you want, if you're willing to be patient, you can find your perfect match via the many amazing rescue facilities around Australia (and the world).

I often daydream and think about the circumstances that ultimately led to Coco and me finding each other. So many variables. It could so easily not have happened. But it was meant to be. If the 'crazy cat lady' alarm bells weren't already ringing, they're about to now, because I can honestly say with hand on my heart that she is the love of my life. That little white fluffball that no one wanted has already given me, and I'm sure many of you, a lifetime of happiness.

And if you want to know how grateful she is that I rescued her, how grateful she is for everything I've done for her, well, the gratitude is written all over her face.

4

Uluru

In my five years as a travelling weatherman I've visited approximately eight hundred towns. That's an average of a couple per week.

I'm calling them 'towns' but many of them are technically cities, suburbs, beaches, islands, caravan parks, mountains, snowfields, resorts, schools, houses, tents. You name it, we've probably visited it.

I knew Australia was big before I took this job, but it's only now that I truly appreciate the enormity of our country. Did you know that to drive from the Gold Coast to Mount Isa takes twenty hours? TWENTY HOURS! And you're still in the *same state*! You'd really want to get along with your Uber driver, wouldn't you?

In the United Kingdom, you can get a train from London and arrive in Paris roughly two hours later. One tenth of the travel time and you've gone international. I mean, the Eiffel Tower is impressive, but have you ever experienced the slides, trampolines and flying fox at the Mount Isa Family Fun Park? I guess my point is nothing great ever comes easy.

Without those wide open spaces, and the hundreds of kilometres of nothingness, I think we'd lose our sense of identity. The outback plays such an integral part in shaping our national character and psyche. Even if you live in the city, you're still connected to the outback. Australia remains that sunburnt country. Only these days with an appropriate splash of SPF 50.

Almost every day someone asks me to tell them my absolute favourite travel destination. They've barely finished asking the question before my face lights up, and I excitedly tell them that it's Uluru. I still get a buzz when someone asks that question. I think it's because I know we're either going to trade Uluru stories or I'm about to put on my Head of Tourism Akubra and borderline bully them into booking their first trip on the spot. I'm extremely passionate about the Red Centre.

I have such a vivid memory of the first time I saw Uluru with my own eyes. I was awestruck. Photographs don't even

come close to doing it justice. The sheer scale and beauty of 'the rock' is genuinely breathtaking. I remember standing there, completely silent, just taking it all in. As most of you probably know, it takes something pretty spectacular to shut me up.

Uluru is in Uluru-Kata Tjuta National Park, so as you enjoy the panoramic views there's nothing but trees, shrubs, rocks and that iconic red dirt as far as the eye can see. Even the drop-off points near the rock can only be accessed by roads that are intentionally winding, to ensure minimal interference. I mentioned above that pictures don't do the rock justice, and neither will these words. You just have to see and feel the aura one day for yourself.

I can close my eyes and be transported back to that first encounter. It was a very hot day. Flies were landing on my face but I barely noticed them. I was completely enamoured with this 550-million-year-old sandstone monolith, towering over outback Northern Territory. The silence. No cars, no buildings, no distractions. It was just me and the rock (and a busload of German tourists).

I'm not a religious person, and I've never considered myself to be overly spiritual. But something about being at Uluru immediately struck a chord with me. There's a spiritual presence, and I found it quite moving.

Like most Australians, I feel an element of shame for how our First Nations peoples have been treated. Of course things are slowly improving, and we're in a much better place than we were even fifty years ago, but I know as a country we can be so much better.

I sat with Anangu Elders and listened to their incredible stories about the spirits of Uluru. What a privilege. I watched young children perform a traditional dance. Beautiful. And I marvelled as a group of artists demonstrated the unbelievable skill and concentration required to create a dot painting. Stunning. The more time I spent just watching, listening and learning, the more I understood. I felt the connection to my country, their country, our country, becoming stronger and stronger.

Uluru is a gift. We have a living, breathing gift, and it must be treated with absolute respect.

The colours. Oh my goodness, the colours. They're ever-changing, depending on what time of the day it is. As Australia's fourteenth most popular TV weatherman, I'm proud to say that the weather also dictates the colour scheme. From the traditional terracotta hue to a dark moody grey. At sunset you may be greeted by a spectacular blue or even violet, but my personal favourite is the almost fluorescent orange glow under the harsh morning sun. It's like fire.

A quick scan of the camera roll on my phone reveals that I've taken twenty-eight thousand photos since I started on *Sunrise*. You'd think it'd be difficult to narrow that many down to a favourite. But again, it's pretty easy, and again, the answer is Uluru.

We were shooting a pre-recorded segment where I needed the rock behind me. A storm came through just as we were about to start filming. Suddenly it was wet, windy and the rock looked grey in the distance. We were all quite frustrated as we had taken our time getting to the right spot and if we'd arrived ten minutes earlier it would've looked perfect.

We decided to give it half an hour and see if things improved. The weather system didn't look to be going anywhere. If only we had a qualified weatherman in our team to predict this kind of thing ...

We were close to giving up on getting the shot when all of a sudden the sun broke through the clouds. They began to fade and the beaming sunshine was now hitting the rock. We were delighted. But it got better.

Almost like magic, a gigantic rainbow appeared. It wasn't a weak one where you really have to squint to see it – it was a bright, powerful rainbow with all colours glowing. What happened next is one of the greatest experiences of my life.

The rainbow, now fully formed, landed perfectly onto Uluru. Imagine a rainbow, but the pot of gold at the end of it is the actual rock. Simply breathtaking. That was the moment I took the best photo I've ever taken. Superb. I feel like there was a lesson in this experience too, because a great philosopher once said, 'If you want the rainbow, you've gotta put up with the rain.' Never a truer word spoken. And thank you to Dolly Parton for that wisdom.

I've been lucky enough to visit Uluru four times with *Sunrise*. Every time, it's been completely different. I've flown over it in a helicopter, I've watched it with breakfast at sunrise, I've taken it in over a few beers at sunset, I've admired it from a distance on a Harley Davidson tour, I've even circled it on a Segway. But there was one occasion I bit off more than I could chew. It culminated in me having to be rescued ... I'll tell you about that at the end of this chapter, but first, I want to share a few of my other favourite travel stories.

One of the most popular features The Human Emoji and I have created on *Sunrise* also happens to be one of the simplest. It was called 'Australia A–Z'. We put the call out to suburbs and towns around the country to tell us why we should visit them as part of our Aussie adventure in 2018. We kicked things off in Ararat, Victoria. Then down the road to Ballarat, across to Crafers in South Australia, then Dangar Island in New South Wales, Echuca, Forster, Geraldton, Hervey Bay – you get the idea.

We could never have anticipated how passionate towns would become with their pitches. The local councils saw it as a great opportunity to get a free kick for their region on national television. It was becoming extremely competitive. But we loved it. When some of the towns found out they'd been successful it was like they'd won the Olympic bid. Brilliant.

As we approached the letter X, it suddenly dawned on us that we didn't really have a choice. After conducting our trademark in-depth research (i.e. typing a question into Google) we realised there was only one town in the entire country beginning with the letter X. That town was, and is, Xantippe.

Xantippe is approximately 250 kilometres north-east of Perth in the West Australian wheat belt. In the most recent census survey, the official population for Xantippe was twenty-one. Not twenty-one thousand. Twenty-one. That's roughly how many viewers we had on the pop-up Channel Ten breakfast show *Wake Up*.

Before we reached X we had to deal with the letter W, for which we were in Wagga Wagga. This wasn't ideal logistically. It meant that when we finished the show in Wagga we had to race to the airport and fly to Sydney. Next, we had to fly to Perth. And then the final leg of the journey was a three-and-a-half-hour drive north-east of Perth to Xantippe. That was all in one day. We travelled 3425 kilometres. And people say TV is glamorous.

We only managed a few hours' sleep because the time difference meant our first live cross was at 2.30 a.m. WA time. Ridic.

I remember driving along multiple dirt roads to find this mysterious 'town'. As we pulled up to the location, I couldn't believe my eyes. People! Lots of people. I mean, it wasn't exactly Woodstock, but I very quickly counted over twenty-one people. THE WHOLE TOWN was here. And more people kept arriving. We eventually reached a tally of one hundred and six people! I can confidently claim to have pulled the biggest crowd ever to Xantippe. #Proud.

The surrounding towns simply couldn't believe that we were visiting Xantippe. They were willing to get up in the middle of the night and head 'just down the road' (which we later found out was a ninety-minute drive for some of them) to be part of 'Australia A–Z'.

What can I tell you about Xantippe? Well, it's essentially a couple of wheat farms. And the 'town' has two sightseeing options: the water tank and the rock. As the sun eventually emerged, we climbed the rock for stunning views. Mainly of the water tank. And as great as those landmarks were, I'd probably advise against choosing Xantippe to set up your new sightseeing operation.

But, as is often the case, it was the people who really brought the morning to life. First it was Colleen and Murray, a couple of nomads travelling Australia in their caravan. They'd been watching our A–Z trip with keen interest, noting spots to add to their itinerary, and had driven almost two hours to meet us in Xantippe.

I was inside their caravan interviewing Murray for one of our live crosses when I felt a strange sensation on my head. I turned around to see Colleen using one of those head-massaging devices on me. It felt incredible. I turned to Murray and said, 'I know she's your wife, but what happens in the caravan stays in the caravan, right?'

Next up I met two of Xantippe's more senior residents, Joy and Graham. They were just as lovely as you can imagine an elderly couple named Joy and Graham would be. I don't think it's possible to have Joy as your name and not be a delightful human being. You never turn on the news and hear that 'Police are on the hunt for the criminal whose name is believed to be Joy'. Never! Joy and Graham had lived most of their lives in the area, and they wanted to share the history of Xantippe. They had brought a charming memento with old black-and-white photos and newspaper clippings to show us. It was really beautiful and I was genuinely interested in learning what Xantippe was like fifty years ago. Spoiler alert: it was exactly the same. But that's what I loved about it!

The Human Emoji and I always love getting to know the people we meet, and we want to celebrate them and share their stories with a national audience. But, since they are usually complete strangers, we also want them to feel comfortable and get to know us. We must have succeeded in Xantippe because, as we were wrapping up the show, Joy and Graham handed me some wheat in a sheath. It was like a bouquet of flowers, but it was wheat, to represent Xantippe. Very special. I'm extremely proud to put that little town and its lovely people on the map, literally and figuratively.

Another memorable morning on the show took place in Port Lincoln, South Australia. We stayed the night on a small boat, so that first thing in the morning I could take the plunge and go shark cage diving. Coincidentally, a few days before this happened, there was a viral video from Mexico of a shark somehow getting into a cage while there was a man in it. I must've had more than twenty 'friends' send that to me in the lead-up to my dive. It says a lot about my friendship group, doesn't it? It really put my mind at ease.

There's no guarantee a shark will appear, particularly in the short window that we're live on air. During my first cross underwater I told the audience we were hoping to see a few sharks by the end of the show. It was only after the cross when I checked my phone that I saw multiple people had tweeted me photos of an enormous shark right behind my head during the cross.

As the morning progressed, we were lucky enough to see a few great whites. The most surprising thing about shark cage diving is how calm it is underwater. When we think of sharks we often picture *Jaws*, a ferocious beast in attack mode. My experience was the complete opposite. I remember seeing a school of fish swiftly disband, and then there she was. The ultimate predator. Slowly gliding towards me, just centimetres away. Her beady eyes sizing me up. It felt like slow motion. And then, much like women in a nightclub, she slipped straight past me without the slightest bit of interest.

Another unforgettable morning on the water took place in Hervey Bay, Queensland. We set out on a mission to find whales, but once again there were no guarantees. My strategy to increase our chances was to use some good old-fashioned reverse psychology. I had signs made up for our group with messages like 'I have no interest in whales', 'First time seagull watching', and my personal favourite, 'Netflix and krill'. The thinking was that if we didn't seem interested in whales, they were going to be more likely to approach us. You know, playing hard to get.

I'm sure some of you think that strategy is ridiculous, but the results speak for themselves. We had whales in every single one of our seven live crosses. It got better and better as the morning went on. They were following us, breaching, and even nudging the side of the boat. An unforgettable experience. And, to top it all off, in our final cross a mother and calf were playing just metres from our camera. Perfection.

The boat had taken us quite far from the shore to find the best vantage point, so by the time we made it back to the jetty it was roughly 9.30 a.m. An hour after we finished the show. I noticed a large crowd of people waiting along the wharf. As we edged closer to land the crowd started to cheer. We were trying to work out who they were applauding when I noticed a few *Sunrise* signs, and other signs with my name on them. The Human Emoji, with a confused look on his face, said, 'I think they're here to meet you.' I was genuinely blown away. Locals and holidaymakers who'd been watching the show on TV had congregated, and waited an hour or more, just to say hello to me. It was a very humbling experience.

Some of the kids had drawn Coco and Catra on their signs, there was even a senior lady with an enormous sign that said, 'Marry me, Sam?' The local Channel Seven crew were waiting to film my reaction to the crowd and the whale-watching experience. The grab they used on the local news showed me waving to around a hundred cheering fans and then I turned to the camera and said, 'I feel like I'm Angelina Jolie.'

Waratah in Tasmania is arguably the coldest town in Australia. That's exactly why it was selected for a special feature we were doing on the show called 'Wintervention'. The concept was simple: we'd visit a town that was ridiculously cold, and send a local family on a holiday to somewhere nice and hot, i.e. the Gold Coast.

To make it entertaining for TV, we invited the entire town to enter the competition. But to be an official entrant they had to be there on the morning, with their suitcase packed, ready to leave immediately after the show for the airport.

The town had an official population of around two hundred people. The day we arrived it was minus four degrees Celsius. On the morning of the broadcast it was a balmy minus one. But that didn't stop the locals from lining up for a shot at the holiday. We eventually counted over one hundred people. Half the town had entered the competition.

At 8 a.m. it was time to reveal the winner. I opened a novelty-sized envelope and congratulated a couple named Anne and Tony. They were understandably over the moon. But there was a twist ...

I turned to the crowd and said, 'Oh, one more thing I forgot to mention ... you're all going to the Gold Coast. We are sending the entire town!' The crowd went berserk. Screams, hugs, tears, it was all happening.

I had intentionally wanted to award it to one winner first so it would be a genuine surprise when I told the whole town the twist. It's quite funny watching the video back because when I announce Anne and Tony as the winners, you can see the other faces drop. Then they remember they're on camera so they pretend to be happy for Anne and Tony.

It was such a beautiful little hardworking town, and many of them had never even been to Queensland. I love being a part of doing nice things for good, honest, deserving people.

We celebrated with them all before they hopped on the bus and headed to the airport, and I left Waratah on a high knowing that my title of the low-budget Oprah was still intact.

Now, back to Uluru. As I mentioned at the beginning of this chapter, I've experienced it almost every way possible. Except the base walk. Walking a loop of the entire rock was something I'd thought about doing, but I was always in such a rush with work.

One afternoon at lunch I was talking to a few senior ladies who recognised me from *Sunrise*. They told me they'd walked the rock that morning and it only took them forty-five minutes. I remember thinking that was a lot quicker than I'd expected. But I also thought, well, if a group of senior ladies can do it in forty-five minutes, I should be able to knock it over in half an hour.

So, later that day I put my sunscreen on, chucked on my Akubra and my sunglasses, and headed solo to the rock. It was roughly 5 p.m. so I figured I had at least an hour or two of light. I started the walk. It was beautiful. Again, complete silence. The only sound I could hear was my boots hitting the red dirt along the way.

There's so much detail in the rock when you get up close. And the colours are ever changing. I was loving this simple way of experiencing Uluru.

I checked my phone and realised I'd been walking for an hour. And I wasn't even close to the halfway point.

Something wasn't right. I started to question the information from the senior ladies I'd met at lunch. Had they really completed the base walk in forty-five minutes? Maybe I was just so transfixed by the rock that I was dawdling? Or maybe they were a group of elite power-walking champions having their ten-year reunion?

I started to panic when it got dark. I really started to panic when I noticed my phone battery was on 3 per cent. What on earth had I done?

All of a sudden, the silence was eerie. And when I did hear a noise I presumed it was a snake or a dingo. I couldn't google what kind of snakes were at Uluru because I didn't want to use the remaining 3 per cent of my phone battery. So obviously I just presumed the answer was large poisonous killer snakes. The snakes were probably closing in on me. I started to curse those old ladies.

I was genuinely worried. It was dark. I was alone. I had no idea how to get out of there. You can't just drop a pin for an Uber near Uluru.

I decided I had to keep walking and finish what I'd started. I had no idea how far I was from the entrance. I just kept walking.

I'm not exaggerating, I started to look for comfortable spots where I might have to spend the night. It then dawned on me that I wouldn't be able to call The Human Emoji (no battery or reception) to tell him where I was. I'd miss the next morning's show! I would be the lead story on *Sunrise*! '*Sunrise* weatherman Sam Mac is reportedly missing after an Uluru base walk went wrong overnight. If you have any information as to his whereabouts please contact The Human Emoji immediately. Sam was last seen wearing an ill-fitting Akubra and designer sunglasses.'

All of these thoughts were crossing my mind. In between thoughts of which part of my flesh I'd offer up to the snakes first.

I was roughly two hours into my walk. It was now pitch black and deadly silent. I'm not ashamed to say I was petrified. But I just kept walking. All of a sudden, hope. I noticed an emergency phone on a stick. I picked it up, and it started ringing. I had no idea who it was ringing. Presumably the prime minister?

An ocker voice answered the phone. It was not the prime minister – it was a ranger named Glen. I told him what had happened and apologised profusely. He had a bit of a chuckle and said I needed to walk back about five hundred metres and he'd pick me up in ten minutes. I was safe!

Immediately my thoughts turned to how much money I could make selling my story to *New Idea*: 'Sam Mac's harrowing two hours lost at Uluru, exclusive pictures inside.'

Glen picked me up and explained that the emergency phone is supposed to be for people with injuries or medical conditions, but I wasn't the first and wouldn't be the last to get lost on a base walk at night.

The rock is in a national park and it was almost time for it to close for the night. I would've been locked in! I plugged my phone into Glen's charger and googled 'how long does it take to walk the base of Uluru?' The answer was 'approximately four hours'. Hmmm. I began to suspect those old ladies weren't *Sunrise* viewers at all – they were *Today* show viewers and I was the victim of a savage stitch-up. Well played, ladies.

5

Loretta

I've been fortunate enough to enjoy a career that has genuinely exceeded my wildest expectations. And in some devastating news for my trolls, I feel like I'm only getting started. But my biggest regret, a regret I think about often, is that I've had to sacrifice so much quality time with my family. I've missed countless precious moments that I'll never ever be able to get back: my sister Paula's birthday parties, Mum (Loretta) and Dad's (Sam senior) wedding anniversaries, my niece Ella's concerts, my nephew Bailey's soccer grand finals. The list goes on.

But it's often the little things I miss the most, like giving Mum a hug when I've had some bad news, or a lazy afternoon strumming away on the guitar with Dad.

My parents have never complained. Not once. They've

been nothing but supportive. They know I'm doing what I have to do to follow my dreams. I think they also know that if they did complain, it would only make it harder for me.

There are definitely times when I worry I'm being selfish. Giving up all of those family moments just so I can chase my career. I've grappled with that guilt. I've questioned whether it's all worth it. Thankfully, the answer is generally a resounding yes. I love what I do. I'm being true to who I am. And I'm making my family proud. Except when I get naked on TV. I think they tell people they're James Tobin's parents when that happens.

This is a story that will tell you everything you need to know about my family.

It's the lead-up to Christmas 2016. My first full year as the *Sunrise* weatherman, what a year! I've taken over a hundred flights, driven tens of thousands of kilometres, visited ninety-two Australian towns, broadcast the show from five different countries, hosted eight episodes of *Best Bits*, a comedy show filmed on weekends in Auckland, and I even found time to narrate a dating show called *First Dates*. It's exhausting even writing all of that. Undoubtedly the busiest year of my life.

That relentless schedule meant I only managed a handful of very rushed catch-ups with Mum and Dad throughout the year. And with only four days planned in Adelaide for

Christmas, even my festive period was going to be rushed. So I decided to surprise them with a very special gift.

We're at my sister's place in Tea Tree Gully for Christmas Day. Now, in case you're wondering just how Irish my family is, I can reliably inform you that our Christmas lunch included roast potatoes, mashed potatoes, baked potatoes, potato wedges and, of course, potato salad. I'm not joking. Potatoes five ways. The great potato famine of the 1800s obviously instilled a belief in the Irish that they must collect and eat *all the potatoes*. My family eats so many potatoes that when we finish Christmas lunch we have to start peeling potatoes again in preparation for the *next* year's Christmas lunch.

Most people will tell you that Christmas is all about family. That's not true. It's about presents.

Paula and I can be quite competitive. So the crown for best present-giver is highly coveted in our family. My sister and I often jokingly (but not really jokingly) ask Mum and Dad who their favourite child is. The response is always the same: 'We love you both equally', because that's what parents are trained to say. I'm not buying it. And I'm a little worried that I've slipped in the rankings over the past decade or so. Not only has Paula spent more time with Mum and Dad, she's also given them two beautiful grandchildren. I've given them two rescue cats.

So, on this Christmas in 2016, I hand the gift to Mum. She says the same thing she says every year when opening a present: 'Oooh, I wonder what it is? Oooh.'

She tears away the last bit of wrapping paper and reveals the gift. It's a *Christmas with André Rieu* CD. Mum and Dad seem a little confused. At no point have they ever expressed any interest in the music of André Rieu.

'Do you like him?' I ask.

Mum responds overenthusiastically, 'Yes, yes, yes,' her pitch heightening with each 'yes'.

I'm revelling in the awkwardness, because I know the André Rieu CD is not the actual present. I let it linger in the awkward zone for another twenty seconds or so, then I offer a suggestion: 'Maybe open the case just to make sure the CD is in there?'

Mum proceeds to open the case. As it clicks open I see the expression on her face slowly change. She then reads out the message I've written on the card: 'Mum and Dad, you're going to Ireland.'

Dad is shaking his head in disbelief; he jumps off the couch and gives me a big hug. My mum is bursting with excitement, but still manages to make a very Loretta-style comment: 'Oh, I'm going to need a new suitcase, Sam.'

Let me explain why this present is more than just a holiday. Despite both of my parents being Irish, they

actually met in Adelaide. Dad left Ireland by himself as a skinny, long-haired eighteen-year-old. And Mum left Ireland on the six-week boat journey to Australia with her family when she was just fifteen.

They were part of a mass exodus from Northern Ireland in the late sixties, seventies and eighties due to an ethno-nationalist conflict known as 'The Troubles'. It was effectively a low-level war. My parents both knew people who were injured or killed. Car bombs, stabbings, shootings. It was ruthless, bloody and dangerous. In an act of desperation, their families both had the same idea: do whatever it takes to get the kids out.

I always sensed a feeling of unease when I asked them about it. Much like they were war veterans. I distinctly remember Dad saying things like, 'I left The Troubles behind', 'I came here to start a new life', and 'I don't need religion anymore'.

In the past few years, however, I'd noticed a shift. It felt like time had healed some wounds. Ireland was also a much safer place. For the very first time, Mum and Dad were actually entertaining the idea of returning to the motherland. There didn't seem to be any rush though – more than forty years had passed and they would still only ever commit to visiting 'one day'!

I was worried that day wouldn't come. They never said this to me, but I think the major roadblock preventing their return was money. My parents aren't wealthy. They have a lovely house in a nice suburb, but they live a very modest lifestyle and every dollar is accounted for. That's how I was raised. So as soon as I had the opportunity to send them on the trip, I took it.

Mum and Dad were scheduled to depart for their trip of a lifetime in March, and as that date drew closer I could feel their excitement building. They were buzzing. Imagine being away from your homeland for almost half a century. The anticipation was electric. Mum was printing tour information, Dad was researching which pubs were still standing. It was the only thing they would talk about, and I loved it.

Finally March arrived. I was in Adelaide for work four days before their departure so I took them out for our last supper at the Royal Oak Hotel. We had a few drinks and Mum ran me through the itinerary in excruciating detail. I'm really happy for you, Loretta, but I don't need to know whether you're doing the 45-minute boat tour or the one-hour boat tour. And despite being a weatherman, I'm not the best person to advise you on whether to take your woollen gloves or your leather gloves. Take both! And just hit me with the highlights please.

We said our goodbyes and I left the pub with a spring in my step. First, because I could feel their excitement and I loved seeing them planning this adventure as a team, and second, because I knew that I'd be going with them.

Even during that initial moment on Christmas Day, in the back of my mind I was hoping I'd be able to join Mum and Dad on the trip. I decided not to say anything, though – I didn't want to get their hopes up. My work schedule is highly unpredictable. Thankfully my executive producer, Michael Pell, was very understanding, despite not wanting me to take leave during a tight ratings battle. He approved nine days, which was enough time for me to go for it.

Now for the second twist (because this story doesn't have enough twists). A few weeks prior to the trip I'd had a sudden moment of realisation: I had to bring Paula.

I remember standing in Hyde Park, Sydney, and calling her: 'Paula, I want you to come with me on this trip to surprise Mum and Dad. I'll pay for everything, you just need to say yes and jump on the plane. I really want this to be a family holiday.'

I was very excited. Paula was understandably nervous. We have completely different lives. I fly every second day, I live a fast-paced life by myself in Sydney, whereas Paula got married young, she has two kids, she's never been overseas and she lives a peaceful life in beautiful suburban Adelaide.

She had some reservations: 'I'm scared of being on a plane for that many hours, and I've never been away from the kids for more than a few days,' she said.

I told her to talk to her husband, Dave, about it overnight and I'd call her in the morning. I finished my pitch by saying, 'Don't you want to see Mum and Dad's faces as they return to Ireland? We will never get an opportunity to do this as a family ever again.'

Bright and early the next morning I called Paula; she answered within one ring, 'I'm in.' Boom! This made me so happy.

Now we just had to deal with the slight problem of Paula not having a valid passport. Thankfully my dear friend Sherief works for the Department of Immigration and he guided her through the process to secure a New Zealand passport (she was born there) in what has to be record time of just over a week.

I called Mum and Dad on the day of their flight to London, as they were beginning their trip in England. I told them to be safe and make the most of every second. I finished the chat by saying I wished I could be there with them and that I couldn't wait to see the photos. I said all of this knowing full well I'd be seeing them over there in a couple of days. It was quite concerning how good I was getting at blatantly lying to my loved ones. Psychopathic tendencies much?

Paula and I had a wine in the airport lounge then took our seats for the flight to London. The plan was to surprise Mum and Dad there then fly with them to Ireland the following day. My parents were spending time with my aunty, Sally, and family, so we had regular updates on their movements. I felt like the affordable James Bond.

As the big surprise drew closer, Paula and I had a last-minute argument over how to execute the reveal in the London hotel where Mum and Dad were due to check in. She wanted us to surprise them together, but I wanted to do two separate surprises. If there's one thing I've learnt in media, it's to milk moments for all their worth. Squeeze out every last little drop. Then squeeze some more. 'Strawberry Kisses' and 'Half Man, Half Cat', anyone?

Eventually Paula accepted my plan, after I gave her a gentle reminder about who was funding her holiday.

Mum and Dad arrived and were approaching the check-in desk. Another thing I've learnt in media is to commit to your ideas. So I should point out that by this stage I was dressed in a borrowed concierge outfit complete with badge and hat. I was also wheeling an oversized trolley. Probably unnecessary detail, but the beauty is in the detail.

I swiftly stroll towards Mum and Dad who are waiting in line. I then say, in a questionable Irish accent, 'May I take your bags, please?'

Mum turns around and her eyes nearly pop out of her head. She does one of the all-time greatest double-takes. In fact, that doesn't do it justice – it was more of a quadruple-take. Once more, Dad is shaking his head in disbelief and, I imagine, a little embarrassment as they've been fooled again. We hug, we laugh, we cry. Perfection.

We check in to the hotel and head upstairs for a drink. We still have part two of the surprise standing by. I take everyone's drink orders then I head to the bar. I quickly explain the situation and my plan to the barman. He looks at me like I've escaped from an asylum. Yet he agrees to cooperate. Probably because he caught a glimpse of the concierge badge I am still wearing.

By this stage, Paula is only fifteen metres away from the group. She's hiding her face behind a menu. When the drinks are ready, she discreetly walks to the bar and picks them up as arranged. Mum and Dad are still processing the fact that I'm with them on the other side of the world when they hear a voice say, 'Anyone for drinks?' Mum and Dad both freeze. Boom. We got them again!

There are hugs and screams and this time Dad's face shows less disbelief and more of a borderline angry expression. He doesn't know who to trust anymore. Glorious.

Loretta retells that moment from her perspective. 'I thought, that waitress sounds like Paula. Oh, that waitress looks like Paula too. Oh, that waitress *is* Paula!'

We clink drinks and explain how we executed our elaborate plan. We're all over the moon and can't wait to head to Ireland as a family the next morning. I feel such a relief knowing that we can finally tell the truth again. And Paula, if you're reading this, I told you two surprises are better than one.

I knew travelling with the family would be memorable, but I dramatically underestimated how hilarious it would be. I don't think I've ever laughed so hard in my life. My parents are not seasoned travellers, so watching them negotiate modern technology in a foreign country was like watching real-life Encino Man.

On the flight to Ireland we all sat in a row. It gave me a chance to hear about Mum and Dad's holiday so far. I asked Dad how he'd found the long flight from Australia.

'It was pretty good. I watched *Hacksaw Ridge* four times,' he said.

'Four times?' I responded. 'You must've really liked it.'

Then Dad said, 'No, it just kept playing on a loop.'

Oh my. Dad didn't realise that the in-flight entertainment system actually had a selection of movies. On a brighter note, if there's ever a *Hacksaw Ridge*–related question at a trivia night, Dad will be all over it.

Loretta was also in fine form throughout the holiday. Unfortunately she hadn't quite mastered her new digital camera ahead of the trip. When I had a flick through her camera roll, we realised that she had captured an entire day of sightseeing with the fish-eye lens setting selected. So if anyone is interested in some fish-eye lens photos of Big Ben, Buckingham Palace etc., please enquire within. They're rather artistic.

Dad didn't exactly nail his sightseeing photos either. Apparently he didn't need a fancy digital camera. He decided that the only camera he needed for this overseas trip of a lifetime was the one on his Alcatel OneTouch phone. This phone is from the early 2000s. It's a museum piece. Its main selling points are the game Snake and AM radio. So picture Dad aiming this phone downwards to capture a shot of the iconic River Thames. I've seen the photos, and it just looks like someone spilt soy sauce on the lens. Or maybe the joke's on me? Maybe he's teaming up with Loretta and her fish-eye project to create their own abstract photography exhibition.

I can't explain how satisfying it felt for Paula and me to be sitting next to Mum and Dad as they touched down on Irish soil for the first time in over four decades. It was very emotional.

We collected our bags and caught a taxi to the hotel. Once we were inside Dad said, 'I could barely understand a word that guy was saying.' He was referring to the thick accent of our Irish cab driver.

I said, 'Yes, that's how everyone feels in Australia when you talk, Dad.'

We checked into the hotel and I witnessed one of the greatest Loretta moments. Mum is famous for dropping a few unexpected doozies. Like when she asked what time *The 7.30 Report* was on. Or the time she was wishing me a fun night at the Logies but instead wrote 'Have a wonderful night at the Oscars'. But even by her standards, this one was a cracker.

We were getting set up in the hotel room and the concierge unfolded a luggage rack. Mum then proceeded to have a seat on the luggage rack and say, 'Thank you very much,' to the concierge. We burst out laughing, then explained to her that it was actually where her suitcase was meant to sit. Classic Loretta. Chef's kiss comedy.

One of the best days of the trip was spent at the world-famous Guinness Factory. We took the tour as a family. When you complete the tour and reach the top level, you enjoy a complimentary Guinness with panoramic views of Dublin. Spectacular. But just the one Guinness was not enough. We're Irish. So we decided to head to the main bar for a few more.

The drinks were flowing and the band was playing a collection of traditional Irish songs. I have a vivid memory of one song in particular: arm in arm, and as a family, we sang 'Wild Rover', a jaunty Irish classic.

I had one of those out-of-body moments. I knew at the time how special that experience was. All of the planning, all of the lying, had been worth it, even for this one moment of musical bonding as a family.

As I get older, I understand more who I am, and how I became who I am. So much of my identity comes from Sam senior. Dad played in bands and is an extremely musical person. I got that from him. Dad is a larrikin, constantly pushing jokes too far. I got that from him. And Dad lives and breathes soccer. I got that from him.

Oh, and just when you thought I couldn't possibly inherit anything else from my dad, I was blessed with his enormous nose. I swear I won 100-metre sprints in primary school purely because of my nose. My nose would finish 2.5 seconds before the rest of my body. However, I still only have the third biggest nose at Channel Seven. The dubious honour of biggest nose at Seven is currently a joint title held by David Koch and Basil Zempilas. I hope that revelation doesn't put their noses out of joint. Slim chance of that – structurally, they're very sound.

My other qualities come from my mum. Kindness and manners. They sound simple, but Mum drilled those two into me right from the start. And she continues to remind me to this day. Thank you, Mum. See, I'm even using manners in this book. Well trained.

My passion for causes such as mental health and animal rescue comes straight from the heart. Straight from Loretta. And Loretta is the type of person who would never say a bad word about anyone. Unless they post a nasty comment about me on Facebook. In which case they should prepare for a savage Loretta smackdown. She ain't playin'.

The eight days in Ireland flew by extremely quickly. Mum and Dad would be staying on for another month, but I had to head back to work. I still managed to squeeze in one more surprise before I left.

Dad is a lifelong Manchester United fan, as am I. We'd never seen them play an English Premier League game live in person. They happened to be playing Arsenal while we were in London. I told Dad that there was a great pub with a big screen that we could watch the game on. We settled into the pub, and Dad was very happy with the situation.

'The beers are cheap, and that screen is huge,' he said. As kick-off got closer, I dropped an Arsenal season ticket onto the table. I'd borrowed it from a friend. Dad looked at the pass, then looked at me, and then once again did his trademark headshake of disbelief.

'We're going to the game, Dad,' I said.

The walk into the stadium with Dad is another memory that stays with me. I can see it as clear as day. We were almost skipping we were so excited. We'd watched thousands of hours of these players on TV in the middle of the night, and now we were about to see them live in the flesh in broad daylight. It was surreal. It felt like a movie, until Arsenal beat us 3–1. It may have been a blessing though, as our borrowed tickets were in the Arsenal fans' section and I doubt Dad would've managed a believable poker face had United won.

Life is short. You have to take control and be a doer. This trip reaffirmed for me that you have to take risks and have a crack. If your intentions are true, everything will work out in the end. Live life for the stories and show people how much they mean to you.

I don't think I ever even looked at how much that trip cost. Because it was irrelevant. There will always be money. But there won't always be an opportunity to sing a song arm in arm with your family in Ireland.

That trip was unquestionably the best thing I've done in my life. When I catch up with my family and someone starts talking about it, their eyes and faces light up. It's joyous.

My parents have made so many sacrifices for me. They've also given me so much knowledge and confidence and ambition. They equipped me to follow and achieve my dreams, so it meant the world to me to be able to repay just a tiny bit of what they've done for me. And even more importantly, I'm doing my bit to keep André Rieu at the top of the CD sales charts.

6

Emoji

Over the past five years, there's one person I've spent more time with than anybody else, and that person is my producer, Sean Flynn, a.k.a. The Human Emoji. I've spent more time with Sean than with my family (and despite the amazing time we had in Ireland, I think they prefer it that way).

We'll get to the nickname in a moment, but first I need you to understand just how intimate our working relationship is. Every morning at 5 a.m. Sean's face is the first I see. Every live cross during the show, he's standing with a clipboard behind the camera. Every flight I take, he's never more than two seats away (both of us in economy, for the record – did you hear that, Kochie?). Every pub meal, he's sitting across the table. Every rural motel, he's in the room next door. Every single step of the way, there he is, right next to me. The Human Emoji. And when we're not physically working together he's chasing me on email, text, phone calls and Insta DMs. I'm considering a restraining order.

I remember my first conversation with Sean very clearly. It was a phone call and he was sharp, warm and professional. Sean is one of those people whose voice doesn't really match his appearance; I believe it's a condition known as DBS (David Beckham Syndrome). So when I met him for the first time in person, I have to admit that I found his appearance quite comical. I don't mean this as a put-down – I've said all of this (and much, much worse) to his face. But I vividly remember seeing him and just smiling at this cartoon-like caricature of a human. Sean is approximately five foot six and has a perfectly circular and shiny bald head. He wears black-framed glasses and oozes charisma.

That first time we met I went very quiet, taking a moment to process my new producer. There he was, bursting with energy, ridiculously expressive in every story he shared like he was on a Broadway stage, his hands flailing all over the shop like a baby penguin that's just discovered its wings. He's quite the spectacle.

Days after meeting Sean I was scrolling through emoji options on my phone, for something completely unrelated, when I stumbled across the smiling-bald-man-with-glasses emoji. It was him! Everything about it just screamed Sean: the overly enthusiastic smile, the perfectly spherical head, the black framed glasses. It was like that emoji was modelled on Sean. The only inaccuracy was that the emoji's skin complexion was more of a yellow tone – but if Sean ever gets jaundice …

So from that moment on I decided that Sean would be known as The Human Emoji. Some people who don't understand our friendship would say, 'Isn't that cruel?' But I see it as a compliment. That emoji is a warm, happy, friendly presence, much like Sean. It brings people joy, much like Sean. I mean, it's not the only nickname I have for him. Over the years I've also referred to him as 'Mr Sheen', 'Rehab Sinéad O'Connor', 'Kochie's illegitimate son', 'Moby' and, probably most offensively, 'Bespectacled Gollum'. Trust me, he got off lightly with 'The Human Emoji'.

Sean is simply outstanding at his job. You can tell because not many presenters dedicate an entire chapter of their book to their producer. Unless it's regarding a bitter court case. And we're probably still a few years away from that.

I don't think one chapter will do Sean justice, but I want to give you a taste of how incredible this man is. If any of my segments over the years have made you laugh or cry, or something in between, The Human Emoji deserves just as much credit as I do. He's the engine room of *Sunrise* Weather. He works tirelessly to get the best out of every guest, in every segment, in every show. He has the most extensive 'little black book' I've ever seen. Suggest a topic and he has multiple contacts for it. Water polo players? Knitting groups? Kamahl? You name it, he's got it covered.

In my first week on *Sunrise* the team had a number of surprise stunts lined up for me. I'm not the most extreme guy and the idea of having to do a whole lot of stunts made me feel slightly uneasy. But that was when the other side of Sean's personality kicked in. Sean is very perceptive, and highly compassionate. He sensed my discomfort before the first stunt and he said, 'I will never ask you to do anything

that I wouldn't do myself.' I'd never had a producer say that to me in my life.

So then, sure enough, when he asked me to bungee jump on my first day, an hour before my live cross The Human Emoji was flying through the air, dangling on a piece of rope, and squealing at a higher pitch than most nine-year-old girls. He was true to his word. What a guy. Trust gained.

One of the most important traits I look for in a producer is a can-do attitude. As a creative person I'm much more likely to share ideas in a supportive environment. If my producer is constantly giving me reasons why I can't do something, and is acting as a creative roadblock, I'm less inclined to share my biggest, wildest ideas.

Sean is the epitome of a producer with a can-do attitude. And if, for some reason, we can't do something, 99 per cent of the time he'll be armed with an adequate alternative or a compromised version of the idea.

Another extremely valuable skill that the best producers have is ingenuity. The Human Emoji excels in this department. I have countless examples of Sean miraculously making things happen against the odds – but I only have room here to share a few of my favourites.

It's Bastille Day 2018, and we're at Sydney's Circular Quay celebrating everything we love about French culture.

The eight o'clock cross is one of our prime-time slots, when we generally aim to put out the strongest content of the day. As per our run sheet, I had already told our viewers that our eight o'clock cross would feature a mime artist.

At 7.58 Sean was nowhere to be seen. Very out of character for him. There was also no sign of the mime artist. I called Sean but he didn't answer. We were now racing against the clock and I was starting to get worried. Live TV waits for nobody, and I had the control room in my ear: 'Coming to you in thirty seconds, Sam.'

Suddenly I hear an out-of-breath Human Emoji in the distance, calling, 'Sorry, we're coming!'

I look up and see a clearly flustered Sean and our French mime artist. Talk about cutting it fine! I didn't even get a chance to meet or chat with the mime artist before we were live on air together.

The segment was fun. Our guest did the classic mimes of opening a door, pulling a chair out and pouring me a glass of wine. I told the viewers that I felt very comfortable around mime artists because I was used to complete silence after most of my jokes. After a couple of minutes I threw back to the studio hosts and we were done. Successful segment.

Once we were off air I asked Sean where he'd disappeared to, and if he realised how close he was to missing the cross.

He told me that the mime artist never arrived. I said, 'Yes, he did, we just did the segment with him, what are you talking about?' Sean went on: 'Umm, that guy was actually a model. We were running late because I had to take him into the office and give him a five-minute crash course in how to do mime. And to make sure it was convincing enough, I then put him in the striped shirt and beret.' I burst out laughing. Rather than accept defeat and just do a short segment focused on the weather, Sean had politely bullied some poor model into launching his mime career live on national TV. It tells you everything you need to know about The Human Emoji. And now he can add mime instructor to his long list of hidden talents.

Another seemingly small, but rather symbolic, example of Sean going above and beyond happened in Adelaide just days before the 2019 Logie Awards, when I was up for the Gold Logie. Adelaide was the final stop of our '5 cities in 5 days' national campaign tour. To celebrate my nomination for the Gold, we'd decided to do a little event in each state. (I'll discuss the Logies experience in more detail later in the book. Spoiler alert: I didn't win.)

The night before the show in Adelaide, I messaged Sean and asked if he could have a gold envelope ready for me to use the next morning. I'd decided to take my mum as my plus one to the Logies, and I wanted to surprise her with that news live on air by handing her a gold envelope with the official invitation.

The next morning at the eight o'clock cross I was interviewing my mum, Loretta, and my sister, Paula. Towards the end of the chat I said, 'As a Gold Logie nominee, I'm allowed to bring a plus one to the event this Sunday on the Gold Coast, so I should probably tell you who I'm taking, shouldn't I, Mum?' Loretta nodded and enthusiastically said, 'Yes, Sam, who's your date?' To which I responded, 'You!' and I proceeded to hand her the gold envelope. The crowd cheered, Loretta's face was beaming with excitement and disbelief. A precious moment.

It was only hours after the show, once we were at the airport, that Sean revealed how stressful the previous night had been.

'I couldn't find a bloody gold envelope anywhere in Adelaide!' he said.

'Well, you found one in the end, so nice work,' I replied.

Then I noticed a menacing grin on his face. He confessed what had really happened: 'So I didn't find a gold envelope. I was getting close to giving up, but in the end I bought a black envelope ... and a tin of gold spray paint!' This just blew my mind. Sean was that hell bent on delivering the gold envelope that he was up at midnight in the shower spray-painting gold onto a black envelope. That is an elite producer. A creative problem-solver. A genius of ingenuity. The Human Emoji always finds a way. Also, apologies to the Ibis Hotel in Adelaide if your shower now has a gold feature wall.

•

I'm the first to put my hand up and admit that I can be challenging to work with. Like anyone, I have days where I'm just not feeling it. The gruelling travel schedule and offensively early mornings can take their toll. And as much as I always try to bring the vibes on air, there are definitely moments when I'm flat. But when your job is to present a national TV show, there's nowhere to hide. There's no flying under the radar. Sean is so in tune with this, and he's a master of finding our balance. He's the yin to my yang. He's a people person, and naturally energetic all the time. Add a few coffees and he comes in like a wrecking ball. He's the perfect hype man. A goggled Flavor Flav. He knows exactly how to fire me up, and even snap me out of power-saver mode when required.

I can also be extremely (some would say annoyingly) particular about certain details. I mean, I'm no Mariah Carey, but I often have a very clear vision of what needs to happen for a segment to work. It's only ever coming from a place of wanting to deliver the best moment on air, the best reveal, the best surprise for the audience. Sean is very understanding of this quirk.

It sounds like I'm talking about my life partner, but he just gets me.

When I first (unknowingly) auditioned for the weather role, Sean had to provide detailed notes to the executive producer of *Sunrise*, Michael Pell. His headline was, 'Sam is determined and extremely ambitious, he brings loads of fresh ideas and he won't change for anyone.' I take that as a compliment. He could see what I was trying to do, and he respected it. And now, after working with me daily for five years, Sean claims that he understands my nuances so well that I could be breathing in a certain way and he knows exactly what I'm about to do. Scary. And slightly creepy.

I initially started name-checking Sean on air as 'The Human Emoji' as an in-joke to amuse myself and the other hosts. But as the years have gone by, he's become a great on-air comedic foil for me. This extends to my social media. I love that most of the audience now know who The Human Emoji is. Producing can be a thankless role at times. All that hard work for less money and less glory. I wanted Sean to be recognised for his contribution. Both on a professional level and on an entertainment level. He's very entertaining.

Sean is the kind of person who will have a go at anything. Before producing the weather, he was in a studio role known as the 'guest greeter'. The most interesting part of that role is that it also involves transforming into THE CASH COW! That's probably the biggest revelation in this entire book: my producer used to be the Cash Cow. Wow – what a demotion for him to now work with me.

Sean claims he was the 'best Cash Cow ever'. He was known for his suggestive Cardi B-esque dance moves and for whispering inappropriate things to the hosts while on camera, e.g. 'Milk me, Samantha, milk me.' But I'd argue that his job is even more bizarre now that he's working with me. Some of the props Sean has had to purchase for my segments include a dog Driza-Bone, ladies' high heels, and a pair of underwear with my cat's face on it. The best part is that he has to send the video of the subsequent live crosses to our accounts department to prove that the purchases were indeed work related. They seem concerned he could be buying these items for his weekend activities.

In his role as producer, Sean has been bitten by a squirrel glider and spat on by an alpaca, and he even once had his 'good jacket' urinated on by a quokka. Yet he's still smiling.

I take particular joy in seeing him become somewhat of a quasi-celebrity. Recently, on a work trip in regional New South Wales, he was doing some private shopping alone at Temora Woolworths when a viewer shouted across the aisle, 'Human Emoji! Let's get a selfie, ya little bugger.' This made me so happy.

Even Kochie, Samantha and the other hosts refer to him as 'Emoji'. Sometimes Sean will be on the phone negotiating a serious work deal when the client on the other end of the line will say, 'Hang on, am I talking to The Human Emoji?'

But the crowning glory happened a few months ago. Sean and I are both big fans of ABC 7.30 host Leigh Sales. I loved her book *Any Ordinary Day* and I think she's a very talented and impressive woman. Imagine my surprise when she plugged my Instagram on her podcast and referred to me as her 'guilty pleasure'. She even told her listeners that my Instagram was 'a community service'.

We started chatting on DM around this time and quickly became Insta pals. One morning in between crosses I was chatting to Sean. We were in Annandale, an inner-western suburb of Sydney, near the iconic Anzac Bridge. I suddenly noticed his eyes darting away, like he was looking past me. I turned around … and there was Leigh Sales! In the flesh! Finally, I was about to meet her. But do you know what the first thing she said was? This is absolutely true: Leigh Sales, arguably the most respected journalist in Australia, excitedly shouted, 'Oh my god, it's The Human Emoji!'

I'd created a monster. Five years of relentless branding had finally cut through in a bigger way than I could have ever imagined.

Leigh then asked to get a photo with The Human Emoji and instructed me to stand awkwardly in the background. *That's my joke, Leigh!* She was giving me a taste of my own medicine. Truly hilarious. After the drive-by meeting she posted the photo on her Instagram with the caption, 'So great to meet a legend of Australian TV, The Human Emoji.' Well played, Leigh, well played.

Sean is so much more than just my producer. He's my biggest supporter, he's my collaborator, he's my counsellor, he's my motivator – and, most importantly, he's my friend. When I'm off work sick he'll drop medication at my door and check in every few hours. We care about each other. It's a rare thing in this line of work. It's schmaltzy, but we were meant to find each other, to work together.

Everything I've achieved in the past five years has been linked in some way to Sean. We celebrate the big wins and crazy adventures together, whether we're releasing a song with The Wiggles or being nominated for the Gold Logie or even lunching with a billionaire. We do it together. But we also support each other through the tough times, whether it's extreme fatigue, or personal issues, or something drastically failing live on air. We live it all together, as a team. And the next day, we get up and do it all again.

Our modus operandi is very simple: 'fun, and with heart'. We're extremely proud of how we make people feel. And we continue to push each other every single day, but always with an underlying respect and appreciation for what we both bring. The magic only happens when we combine our powers. I love you, Human Emoji.

7

111

Here is a list of 111 things I've done in my five years as a TV weatherman:

- I dedicated an entire morning to knitting and attempted to create an east side/west side-style rivalry between the Sydney Knitting Club and the Knitters' Guild NSW. I had them all in stitches.
- I joined the Girl Guides in Marrickville, Sydney. Which I'm quite certain immediately places me on some sort of watchlist.
- I defeated a 93-year-old woman named Barbara at table tennis in the games room of her retirement home. Mercy is for the weak.

- I was taking a photo with the legendary Molly Meldrum and he said, 'Gimme a kiss.' I thought it would make a fun photo so I planted one on his cheek. Turns out he was talking to his dog, Ziggy, who was on his lap.

- I was removed by security at a Shania Twain concert for getting 'too close to the artist'. It was involuntary. She's my spiritual muse. I eventually agreed to my friend Matt Gilbertson writing about the incident in the *Adelaide Advertiser* on the condition he use my suggested headline, 'Sam's absolute Twain-wreck'. #Proud

- I got naked live on TV with two non-English-speaking Japanese men at Kinosaki Onsen. Hey, it can get kind of lonely on the road.

- I failed to catch my first wave in a one-on-one lesson with surfing world champion Mick Fanning. After an excruciating thirty minutes Mick said, 'I've actually gotta go to another meeting.' I also found out after the segment that I was wearing a women's rashie. Yiew.

- I attended Mulletfest at Kurri Kurri in the Hunter Valley. Yes, it's a celebration of the iconic hairdo. It may shock you to learn the eventual winner was a man named 'Shagger'.

- I hired a butt coach in preparation for *The Real Full Monty*. Needed to tighten up my 'Gluteus Sam Macximus'.
- I accidentally pushed a child off a hoverboard in Adelaide's Rundle Mall in 2016. I still think about it daily. I'm sorry, Charlie.
- I commentated strongman Jordan Steffens pulling a Qantas 737 at Adelaide Airport in the pouring rain while Hans the German sang Mariah Carey's 'Hero' despite not really knowing the words. Sometimes a punchline is not required.
- I flew to Auckland every weekend for two months to host a late-night comedy panel show called Best Bits. Or as the Kiwi production company pronounced it, 'Bist Butts'.
- I went for a run with former foreign minister Julie Bishop. She very kindly tolerated me calling her J-Bish.
- I was bitten by an emu at Sydney Zoo while reading the weather forecast. The audience didn't even see it. They just heard me say, 'Sunny and a top of twenty-six for Brisbaaaaaaaaaahhh, I was just bitten by an emu.'
- I was rope-tied to TV's Larry Emdur for thirty minutes. It was part of a challenge morning, but

we're now using it as a pilot for a new show titled *Bondage with the Stars*.

- I once featured as a quiz question on *The Chase*: 'Who became the *Sunrise* weatherman in 2016?' The contestant's answer was, 'Sorry, pass.' It meant she missed out on the cash prize. What a shame.
- I competed in a swimming race against an eleven-year-old girl named Ashana while wearing a full tuxedo. It was commentated by swimming icons Susie O'Neill and Ian Thorpe. They deserve better.
- I discovered an Indian–Italian restaurant in Bright, Victoria. So I proceeded to share their concept with the nation by making them a free advert on *Sunrise*. 'Love Indian? Love Italian? Why not have both? Come to Bright and try the spag-vin (™).'
- I've held fourteen different koalas in fourteen different segments across the country. And can still claim to be relatively chlamydia free.
- I hugged John Travolta! And can still claim to be relatively Scientology free.
- I created the world-first leg-hair beard. It was the Robin Hood of personal grooming: we stole from the rich (my legs) and gave to the poor (my face). And from a safe distance of 4.5 metres it looked just like a regular beard.

- I was bitten by a pig on a beach in Fiji.
- I swam with great white sharks in Port Lincoln, South Australia. They were on the hunt for fur seals. Worryingly for me, I have the exact same physique as a fur seal.
- I raced against a ute travelling at the exact same speed as Usain Bolt's world record time. I might have lost the race, but I think you'll agree it was worth it when I tell you I called the vehicle 'Ute-sain Bolt'.
- In one of the most Queensland experiences ever, I did yoga on the top of Brisbane's Story Bridge with Lincoln Lewis, son of King Wally Lewis. Prime

example of me doing something extremely random on the show purely as an excuse to squeeze in a quick catch-up with a mate. Onya, Lincoln.

- I was transformed into a *Lord of the Rings* dwarf by a prosthetics artist at Weta Workshop. The concerning part was that the 'cartoonish comedic nose' they attached to my face was only millimetres bigger than my actual nose.
- I learnt how to sail in Auckland Harbour. Predominantly so I could hear my Kiwi instructor pronounce 'All hands on deck'.
- I discovered a rock protruding from the ground in the Victorian High Country that was the exact same size and shape of a regular human bum. I very creatively crowned it 'Bum Rock'.
- While in Yarrawonga, Victoria, I hit a golf ball from Victoria to New South Wales! Admittedly it only travelled twelve metres and into a lake, but that's an impressive headline, right?
- I had breakfast with orangutans in Singapore. Very similar to having breakfast with our crew. Only better table manners.
- I lied to music icon Michael Bolton about it being my mum's birthday in order to manipulate him into agreeing to join me in serenading her. In my

defence, I said her birthday was 'coming up'. And it was. Just in eight months' time.

- I climbed through the roof of the Sydney Opera House sails. At the top you open a manhole, poke your head out, and take in the view of the Harbour Bridge. One story, three icons.

- At the annual Elvis Festival in Parkes, New South Wales, I decided to dress as Elvis Costello. I then spent the entire day explaining who Elvis Costello was to confused *Sunrise* viewers.

- I was electrocuted by Sonia Kruger in the *Big Brother* house. Always have a safe word, guys.

- I drank nine different types of sake in one minute at a distillery in Tokyo. It instantly improved my Japanese.

- I was heading up the escalator at the Melbourne Airport Qantas Club when I noticed John Farnham coming down. John Farnham in the wild is like a unicorn sighting. And, in my panic, all I managed to do was wink. I winked at music royalty. I sat in silence, I lived in fear. Whoaooohhhhh. One of my biggest regrets of my time in the role. #Winker

- I had an echidna eat food off my face at Australia Zoo. Hey, it can get kind of lonely on the road.

- I lived out my dream of drinking chocolate straight from the vat at the Haigh's Chocolate Factory. The tap is much more powerful than you think. For legal reasons, they've requested I point out that this experience is not open to the general public.

- We once managed to do an entire morning of crosses from a nude life drawing class without breaching any television codes of practice.

- I was tackled to the ground by the riot police at the Goulburn Police Academy. Again, we forgot to agree on a safe word and my good chinos were ripped in the process. This prompted the #PutYourChinosOut4Sam movement. PS: for future reference, my safe word is 'pineapple'.

- I drove a Formula One car in Dubai. Before discreetly asking the editors to speed up the footage.

- A lady named Tash in Adelaide used a selfie we took as her Tinder profile picture. I'm still confused as to whether that was a compliment or merely an advertisement for how low she's willing to drop her standards.

- I pole danced to the James Blunt song 'Goodbye My Lover'. I see the pole as an extension of myself.

- I water-skied along the Murray River. For approximately 2.8 seconds. But that was long enough to get the shot for the 'gram, which, as we know, is all that really matters in life.
- I stripped down to nothing but a Canadian flag at the Takhini Hot Springs. 'Oh Canada!' Both their national anthem and what people said upon being subjected to this vision.
- In what has to be one of the biggest challenges of my life, I managed to get through an entire segment without laughing, smiling or even sniggering at the fact we were going live in Tokyo from a place called 'Takeshita Street'. #Proud.
- I took a celebratory swim in the Yarra after winning a table tennis point commentated by Bruce McAvaney. I can still smell it.
- I ate Fergburger for all three meals on my first day in Queenstown, New Zealand. It feels good to say that aloud. Now I can get help, or an Uber Eats endorsement deal. 'Tonight I'll be having the same as I had for breakfast and lunch ...'
- I sat next to former prime minister John Howard on a flight to Perth. Quite fittingly I was sat on the centre left and he was on the right wing. #CuttingEdgePoliticalHumour

- I sang the *A Star is Born* 'Shallow' duet with Hans the German. We still don't know who was Bradley and who was Gaga.
- I competed at the Ride-on Lawnmower Championships in Shepparton, Victoria.
- Kara Simmonds in Bendigo contacted me on Instagram asking me to be in her baby announcement photo. I get some odd requests, but this one took the cake. So, I visited her at work and did a ten-minute photo shoot that included me kissing her bump while holding a handwritten sign that read 'Not the dad'. Important clarification.

- I did my weather crosses from the world-famous Heart Reef off Hamilton Island. I wore a full tuxedo for the occasion. People thought I wore it to look cool, but it was just another desperate attempt to protect my pale Irish complexion from the harsh Queensland sun.
- I was the first Australian male television host to wear 'scrunch bum' workout pants on air. #GluteusSamMacximus strikes again.
- I received a verbal warning from the Disney on Ice team in Wollongong for having 'inappropriate interactions with Princess Elsa'. I'm not a competent ice skater, so the only way to avoid falling was to grab her shoulder slash hair. They really need to let it go. Let it go.
- With the help of Siri reading the weather, and some pre-written cards, I delivered an entire three-minute weather segment without saying a word. It was a challenge from Sam Armytage. The most important card read, 'For too long, us straight white males have not had a voice in mainstream media.'
- I seductively massaged honey into The Human Emoji's head at a birthing class in Sydney. It was consensual.

- My Embarrassing Dad performance of 'Keep on Moving' by 5ive was retweeted by the boy band themselves. That's what success feels like.

- I created an S Club 7 tribute act called S Club 1. Again, my video was reposted by members of the band. This is what happens when you reach for the stars, guys.

- I met one of my idols, Shaun Micallef, at Melbourne Airport. He knew my name! Well, either that or he subtly read it off the tag on my bag.

- I cried three times on a flight to Hawaii during the movie *La La Land*. I cried when he thought she'd only stay with him if he had a secure job. I cried when she thought she wasn't good enough as an actress. And I cried during the musical montage. More like *Sooky Sooky La La Land*.

- I stayed on the rural property of one of the contestants of *Farmer Wants a Wife*. The internet was terrible so I joked to him, 'More like *Farmer Wants a Wifi*.' He smiled politely and I still think it deserved more. So now it's in my book.

- I appeared on the front page of the *Port Lincoln Times*. Yeah, that's a flex.

- I delivered sixteen fish puns in one minute in a live cross from the Sydney Fish Markets. A wonderful day at the office for 'Salmon Mackerel'.
- I tap-danced to the Adele song 'Someone Like You' at Glamour Puss Studios in Melbourne while dressed as a mirror ball and holding a baby doll. I went to university.
- Ally, Australia's strongest woman, attempted to bench press me above her head at Coco's Gym on the Gold Coast. It was all going smoothly until the final part of the lift, when she reached for a stronger grip and her hand landed smack-bang

on my groin. Right there for all to see. I lost my innocence that day. But hey, it can get kind of lonely on the road.

- I visited a cat cafe in Tokyo and learnt the Japanese translation of 'I will die alone surrounded by cats'. I've never felt so accepted and at peace.
- I shook hands with Brian May from Queen. Yassss, Queen!
- I said on air if a particular photo received ten thousand likes I would recreate my highly offensive Year 9 bowl-cut hairdo. It received ten thousand likes within an hour, which makes me think some of the audience really don't like me.
- I did an entire morning of the show with an Auslan interpreter. He blitzed it. At the end I challenged him to sign the 50 Cent song 'In Da Club'. Auslan has never been so gangsta.
- In a brief, drive-by interview with then prime minister Malcolm Turnbull, I asked him if he was a 'Delta or Ricki-Lee man'. He was Team Delta and I stand by the fact that Australia deserved to know. You don't get that on Q&A.
- I performed a choreographed synchronised swimming routine to the Madonna song 'Express Yourself' with the under-12s at the Ian Thorpe

Aquatic Centre. Again, something that probably immediately placed me on a watchlist.

- I was hurdled by Olympic champion Sally Pearson at a Little Athletics club. The following year I repaid the favour and hurdled her back. You haven't lived until you've experienced the gut-wrenching fear that you could be about to kick a much-loved Olympian and new mum in the face.

- I convinced an entire Latin dance school to dance to the Shannon Noll song 'Drive'. A song about a big black shiny car has never seemed so romantic.
- I met the Hilltop Hoods backstage and pitched them my concept for an all-Christian rap group called The Hillsong Hoods. Still waiting to hear back.
- I milked venom from a snake at the Australian Reptile Park. Hey, it can get kind of lonely on the road.
- I had a selfie with former prime minister Julia Gillard at Adelaide Airport. We were at the security checkpoint and I excitedly pointed out that we had the same laptop. They were MacBook Pros so we're hardly soulmates, but I was just trying to establish a connection, okay.
- I interviewed my friend the wonderfully talented comedian Dilruk Jayasinha and decided to give him the greatest name-specific pun he'll ever receive. I told him that instead of jokes he should refer to his one-liners as 'Jayazingers'. The fact that he hadn't already was a 'dilrukie error'. He smiled politely. I haven't seen him since.
- I met Australia's oldest man, 111-year-old Dexter Kruger, in Roma, Queensland. Naturally I collab'd with him in a TikTok video. You know I'm not joking.

- I was incorporated into a routine by a Mongolian contortionist. First time a woman has ever bent over backwards to impress me.
- I went dog sledding through the snow in the Canadian Rockies. As a cat man, it was such a foreign experience to see an animal actually trying to please me.
- I met my comedy hero Conan O'Brien on 21 February 2019 and gave him a hug so long

I could see his security guard beginning to approach. Mid-hug Conan looked at me, with fear all over his face and said, 'Sir, tell me, will I ever see my family again?' It was such an honour to finally meet someone with a paler complexion than me.

- I sang 'Horses' with the great man, Daryl Braithwaite. He asked if we needed backing music. I assured him we'd be just fine to go 'Sam Macapella'. He smiled politely.
- I went to the top of the world's tallest building, the Burj Khalifa in Dubai. Good view, but it's no Adelaide.
- I drank water direct from Lake Tahoe in Nevada. So clear, so pure. I would not recommend trying the same thing in the Yarra.
- I had my G-string auctioned for charity in Western Australia. It was the one I wore for *The Real Full Monty* (not that there's more than one, Your Honour). And, yes, it was washed.
- I've received the bird from Kochie twice while live on air. I take it as a badge of honour. Incidentally, two is how many times the Crows have won the AFL premiership. Double the number of premierships of Port Power.

- I appeared in the 'Spotted' section of *The Daily Telegraph* for buying cat food in IGA. I love that someone thought that was newsworthy enough to bother contacting the paper. #Proud
- I auditioned as the Cowardly Lion in *The Wizard of Oz*. And was apparently 'too cowardly, and too uncoordinated'.
- I arranged for an offensive shirtless thirst-trap selfie my pal Matt Doran took to be displayed on the super screen at Allianz Stadium. The gut was actual size. Love you, Matthew.
- I appeared (or 'feetured') four times on a male foot fetish Instagram page called Mcfeetfacefeety. I was feeling pretty good about myself until I noticed that Osher Günsberg's feet received more likes than mine did. Sole destroying.
- I wrote and performed a song about the small town of Bowna (pronounced 'boner') in the New South Wales Riverina. It included the line 'It's gonna be hard … to leave this place.'
- Seconds before a live cross, I witnessed Sam Armytage's dog Banjo getting an erection. If only this had happened in Bowna.
- I visited 'The Polish Place' on the Gold Coast and did a shot of vodka that contained 95 per cent

alcohol. I later found out there's a warning on the bottle not to drink it straight because it has higher alcohol content than hand sanitiser. I had The Human Emoji drive me back to the hotel that morning.

- In Margaret River, Western Australia, I was granted one question to ask cooking queen Nigella Lawson. In the biz I'm known for my bravery. So I went there. I asked her if she was for or against pineapple on pizza. She was in favour. Again, Australia deserved to know.

- I appeared on the cover of *New Idea* wearing a burnt orange turtleneck skivvy and red thick-rimmed glasses. It's called fashion, bro, google it.

- I played handball against former prime minister Kevin Rudd.

- I sat next to Bindi Irwin on a music quiz show and thought it would be the beginning of a lifelong friendship. The follow-up thank you message I sent her on Instagram has been left on 'seen'. It's been four years.

- I met a redheaded kid dressed like Ed Sheeran at an Ed Sheeran pop-up store in Sydney. He was playing the guitar and I put an Ed Sheeran hat on his head as a present. He freaked out, threw it on the ground, kicked it, tripped over a mic cord and landed on the floor. The segment prompted one of my favourite headlines: 'Ed Sheeran's mini-doppelgänger has a meltdown live on *Sunrise* after Sam Mac tries to gift him a hat.'

- I ate the world's hottest chilli, the Carolina Reaper. Wowsers. Within seconds of it touching my mouth I had lips like a *Married at First Sight* contestant.

- A sponsored campervan with an enormous photo of my face on it was 'accidentally' parked out the front of an adult store in Wagga Wagga, New South Wales, by our crew. For an entire afternoon.

- I went horse riding in the Victorian High Country wearing RMs, a Driza-Bone and an Akubra. I had a piece of rope swung over my shoulder and invited investors for my saucy new movie *50 Shades of G'day*. As yet, no interest.

- I fell off a horse at Rainbow Beach, Queensland, when it decided to exfoliate in the sand. Sorry to interrupt your skincare routine, bro.

- I declined an offer from a mum to be a topless waiter for a fundraiser at Glenelg Primary School. Regardless of the circumstances, taking your clothes off at a primary school is NEVER a good idea.

- I was accused of cheating my way into showbusiness in an article by news.com.au because I'd rorted votes in a radio competition back in 2004. The piece presented a wonderful opportunity to launch yet another, slightly more sinister, alter ego, 'Scam Mac'.
- I once held an umbrella for Matt Damon during a red carpet segment. Arguably the most weather-related thing I've ever done in the role.
- I met ABC TV star Leigh Sales at a park in Annandale, New South Wales. Sounds dodgier than it was. She even suggested *Accidental Weatherman* as a title for this book. It's far more credible than my original idea: *Moist Conditions*.
- I bathed with our sound operator, Wayne McKelvie, in an outdoor hot spring in Rotorua. But, hey, it can get kind of lonely on the road.
- I walked my cat Coco on a pink lead with a diamante-encrusted collar and Swarovski cuffs on her paws. And #Loretta wonders why I'm not married yet.
- I was described by Todd McKenney as 'the worst stripper ever' in the history of *The Real Full Monty*. The most demoralising part was

that in the article they used a photo of Bachelor Matty J's body. My rig wasn't even clickbait-worthy.

- I joined five babies in a spa at a Gold Coast baby day spa. It looked cute and exciting and funny on the TV. But I made the mistake of looking down after the segment and noticed a few different colours in the water. A perfect metaphor for my life as a travelling TV weatherman.

8

Carol

Hi Sam …

I'm actually starting to like you these days, I think you've settled into your role and you are not so annoying now.

Except …….. please chuck out that army fatigue coloured shirt in dirty green. That colour is not T.V. friendly. You suit blue tones and bright greens, not browns, tans or motley green. Okay, I've done my motherly deed for the day. Of course you will say I will wear what I want, go ahead, it just doesn't suit you. Keep smiling, you're growing on me.

Regards, Carol

That was an actual Facebook message I received on 24 January 2019. It's important to point out that this message arrived completely out of the blue – or out of the dirty green. I had never met or heard of this mysterious lady named Carol, but something told me I needed to investigate further.

I remember reading the message and being slightly confused. Was this stranger complimenting me or was she absolutely savaging me? I mean, if they were compliments, they were so backhanded they were forehands. But there were no swear words, no threats, and Carol sounded like the name of a lovely old lady who lived next door and took great pride in her garden.

I immediately read the entire message again, taking time to digest every single word. I suggest you do the same.

After the third read, I burst out laughing. The whole message really tickled me. And there was a lot going on in those short paragraphs, so I started to unpack them.

In the first sentence Carol congratulated me because I was 'not so annoying now', which implied that she found me extremely annoying initially. Thanks, Carol.

Next, she told me the two colours I could wear on the air and three colours I couldn't. So she effectively just appointed herself head of the Channel Seven wardrobe department. Bravo, Carol.

And finally, she wrapped up this emotional rollercoaster by telling me to 'Keep smiling, you're growing on me'. Passive-aggressive much, Carol?

But let's make no mistake: at its core, this message was a targeted attack. And Carol, the smiling assassin, was not going to stop until that dirty green shirt had been banished from my wardrobe.

Receiving unsolicited feedback and criticism from random people comes with my job. It's a daily occurrence. Sometimes it even happens face to face. And some people seem to think that because I'm on TV it's fair game to say whatever they want to me. Often before they've even told me their name.

They say things like, 'You're shorter than I thought', 'You're taller than I thought', 'You're skinnier than I thought', 'You're bigger than I thought', 'You look younger on TV', 'You look older on TV', 'Your nose is bigger in person', etc.

It's true, I once had someone say my nose looked bigger in person. It was the first thing he said to me. Now, he was probably right: I do have a big nose. Or a 'strong nose', as my mum, Loretta, calls it. Aren't mums great?

I also used to get teased at school for having a lot of freckles. But Loretta put my mind at ease by saying 'every freckle is just a little kiss from the sun'. Beautiful.

I'm not precious about this kind of thing; I often find it funny. But there are times when it's definitely rude. It would be like meeting someone via a dating app then seeing them in person and saying, 'Geez, you've got more chins than I thought.' I mean, you can think that, but you don't always need to say it out loud.

As for online feedback ... wowee. It's a jungle out there. I've been called every name you can imagine. I've received actual threats of violence, and I've even been told a handful of times to go and kill myself. It can be really nasty stuff. But those messages say more about the sender than they say about me. If a TV weatherman riles you up that much, maybe just use an iPhone app for your forecast? Or try some meditation, bro.

Occasionally I'll try to understand why I've enraged them so much, and I'll take a look at their profile. The profile is basically the same every time: a guy with a goatee who only posts photos of the 'sik' exhaust on his VK Commodore. His bio is something like 'We grew here, you flew here'. The page will also contain some sort of conspiracy theory about how the government is controlling our minds. And he shares all of this riveting content with his twenty-eight followers. Simple fix for me: block and move on.

I was so enthralled by Carol, on the other hand, that I decided to share a screenshot of her message with my followers on Instagram. It blew up. Almost ten thousand likes and hundreds of comments.

I think it resonated because everybody knows a Carol. She's often an aunty or a friend's mum who happily shares her opinions on *everything*! Whether you've asked her or not.

It's important here that I make the distinction between a Carol and a Karen. Two very different beasts. Karens are troublemakers with no self-awareness. They'll steal your parking spot and laugh about it with their kid. Whereas Carols have redeeming qualities. They're often sweet natured and genuinely well intentioned, which is why their critiques can catch you off guard and cut extra deep.

After reading Carol's message, my followers were quick to jump to my defence and return serve. Ruth commented, 'Shush lady, let Sam be.' Daniela added, 'Carol needs to dial it down a few notches.' Bonnie got a little more personal towards Carol and said, 'She sounds like she would be the mother-in-law from hell.' But there was also a legion of Carol sympathisers, like Liane, who chimed in with, 'It's true, dirty green is such a primary school uniform colour. Vomit. Thank you for speaking up Carol.' Great, now my own Instagram account was divided. It was very quickly becoming Sam vs Carol.

The next morning I was doing the show from Parramatta Park in the lead-up to Australia Day. And if you know me at all, you'll know exactly what colour shirt I was wearing – you betcha, dirty green! I even began each of my seven live crosses by saying, 'Good morning, Carol.' Admittedly, that would've been slightly confusing to people who didn't follow me on Instagram. But it was personal now. And I needed her to know that I wasn't backing down.

I even showed Carol's message and discussed it on air with the rest of the team. Now the whole of Australia knew who Carol was. This saga was gaining some real momentum. But something was missing ...

Everybody knows it's not a legitimate saga until there's an official hashtag. So I launched #PutYourDirty GreensOut4Carol. I encouraged viewers to wear the colour dirty green and send me a photo using that hashtag. Yet again, an unbelievable response. Hundreds of photos within an hour. Some of my favourites included a lawyer wearing a dirty green scarf to work despite it being the middle of summer. Footy teams who had dirty green uniforms using it as an excuse to rep club colours at work. And I even had a lady send me a bedroom shot of her in a matching dirty green underwear set. She was putting her dirty greens out, all right.

By this stage I was wondering how Carol was going to react to her newfound fame. Sure enough, right on cue, not long after the show, I received this message:

Hi Sam …

Thank you for saying good morning to me on *Sunrise* today. I will be a celebrity at the leisure centre now. I am liking you even more. But remember, the green shirt is not for you. It's worse than the khaki. Blue shirt next week to suit your twinkling smile. Hehe.

Regards, Carol

She doubled down! It had become very apparent that Carol was relishing this battle. She was as cool as a cucumber (cucumbers are, coincidentally, dirty green). Then it dawned on me: I had met my match. I was legitimately being trolled by a chardonnay-sipping, bob-cut-sporting senior citizen named Carol who lives in a Central Coast retirement village. What a time to be alive.

Over the next few days, I mentioned Carol regularly on the show. I was also receiving countless messages from other viewers asking if Carol approved of my shirt colour, or if Carol had sent me any new fashion critiques. The in-joke had become an out-joke. Excellent. You have to reach a certain level of fame before you can be instantly recognisable for your first name alone, but that's what had happened. Beyoncé, Mariah, Carol.

The Human Emoji and I knew exactly what had to happen next. It wasn't an easy one to get over the line with the powers that be, but we kept pushing and pushing, and eventually we got the (dirty) green light to do the show live from the Central Coast leisure centre where I could meet my new nemesis, Carol, live on air.

I remember Friday, 7 February 2019 like it was yesterday. At 3.07 a.m. my alarm is buzzing. But so am I on a day like this. I leap out of bed with a spring in my step. The absurdity of what we're about to do genuinely excites me. These are the days I live for.

On the ninety-minute drive to the coast my body is full of the kind of nerves you only normally get before a first date. In many ways, this is a first date. Only, Australia will be watching …

I arrive at Valhalla Lifestyle Village twenty minutes before my first cross. Wow, I must be excited, because that's uncharacteristically early for me. The Human Emoji and I converge in a quiet side street away from the action so we can concoct a plan. We agree that Carol and I should meet for the first time live on air. We want the audience to see our actual meeting, not a fake, rehearsed TV meeting. Again, pushing for authenticity.

Next, Sean and I have a five-minute conversation about whether or not it's socially acceptable to put a blindfold on a senior woman purely to add drama to a reveal. The decision is unanimous: Carol will be blindfolded.

Before the big reveal, I am hiding behind a shrub. A dirty green shrub. I have my earpiece in, listening to the show, so I know exactly when to emerge.

This gives me a private moment to really appreciate how ridiculous my job is. A couple of weeks ago a lady wrote a random message to me on Facebook about the colour of my shirt. And now here I am at her retirement home, about to meet her for the first time, with hundreds of thousands of viewers across the country coming along for the ride.

I trusted my gut with this storyline. If you took a few of Carol's quotes in that original message out of context you could be forgiven for thinking she was attacking me. And some people did think that. But there was also warmth in that message, and it made me think she wasn't just another troll – she had strong opinions, but she also had a very funny turn of phrase. This made me believe she'd be great talent. Well, we were about to find out.

'Five, four, three, two, one, yeahhhhh ...' The Human Emoji removes Carol's blindfold. Our crowd of seniors goes berserk, cheering, whistling and whooping. It's like schoolies for old people. I'm wearing a dirty green headband, dirty green socks, dirty green sleeveless army jacket and the star of the outfit: a fluoro-green Lycra full-body morph suit. Hello, ladies.

Carol is in complete shock. Or she's dirty green with envy. We give each other a big hug. I start to interview her about her newfound fame when I notice her gazing down towards my business section.

'My eyes are up here, Carol,' I say. The crowd laughs. Carol pats my hips.

I'm normally very good at keeping it together on the air, but there is something about this whole scenario that is making me laugh uncontrollably. It is completely preposterous that a huge TV network would put time, money and resources into doing an entire show from a retirement village all because a lady named Carol complained about the colour of the weatherman's shirt. Perfection.

Carol lived up to all the hype. She was friendly and funny and sweet, but she also had a sinister side to her that could cut people down with just a few words from her acid tongue.

In the next cross we were live from Carol's house. We sat down on her couch and discussed all of the breakfast TV shows. Sadly for the ABC, it wasn't a glowing review.

'No, that show's no good,' said Carol, 'Virginia Trioli talks over people too much.'

I opened the door to Carol's study, where she had a desk and a laptop. I labelled it her 'trolling office'. Nobody's safe when Carol is on the case.

I asked if we could show our viewers her bedroom. Carol's husband, Phil, said, 'We'd better hide the toys first.' Wow. This was wild!

I opened Carol's wardrobe and gave her a taste of her own medicine, pulling out garment after garment and telling her that the 1980s needed their shoulder pads back.

Sean did an incredible job that morning. He backed me and it paid off with some outrageously memorable and feel-good TV. I still have people mentioning how much they enjoyed that morning's show, even years after the fact.

The Human Emoji went above and beyond by arranging some gifts for me to present to Carol before we left. The first was Carol's face on a T-shirt and the words 'Keep smiling, you're growing on me'. The second was a coffee mug with the inspirational quote she dedicated to me at the beginning of this entire adventure: 'You're not so annoying now.'

I ended the morning by serenading Carol with a version of the classic Everly Brothers song 'All I Have to Do Is Dream'. It went like this:

When I want you, my judgey friend
When I want you … to slide …
Into my DMs
Whenever I want you
All I have to wear
Is gree-eeen, green green green

The whole village joined in as back-up singers. At the end of the song I went to give Carol a kiss on the cheek, but she had other ideas. Live on air she changed the angle of her face at the last second and planted one on my lips. It might have been the only action I would get that year …

I still keep in regular contact with Carol. I should probably sell my story to *New Idea*: 'How I befriended my online troll.' I know I can always count on Carol to tell me which segments I nailed and which segments I failed.

She seems to be at peace with my wardrobe these days. For now, at least. And when I was up for the Gold Logie later that year, as a special nod to Carol I wore a custom-made velvet suit, in dirty green, to the awards ceremony. I found that more satisfying than you'll ever know.

But all jokes aside, I think people should wear what makes them happy. Don't dress for others – dress for you. That's my Oprah-style editorial for the day.

Carol now has actual fans. People ask me about her often. There's a genuine affection towards her. Some of my followers comment on my posts with the #TeamCarol hashtag. I love it. The tide has well and truly turned.

Kelly wrote, 'I love Carol and her sass, yass kween!' Toney gave me a word of warning: 'Never mess with a Carol or a Susan, Sam.' Lisa articulated why this whole thing really struck a chord: 'I'm so invested in this, there's a little bit of Carol in all of us.' Hayley seemed to have adopted Carol as some sort of mentor: 'is cazza available to do a personal run down on where i need to improve because i'm ready for a wake up call.' And Lucy fell in love with Carol: 'Ahhh, I wish she was my friend, bless her and her khaki socks.'

Even *Sunrise* host Sam Armytage seemed to have joined #TeamCarol. She once finished a segment by saying, 'I agree with Carol – you're not so annoying now.' Gee, thanks.

The final word in this story, though, has to go to the great Carol Embleton. A few days after I visited her she sent me another direct message. This one made me suspicious that perhaps she knew exactly what she was doing the whole time, and maybe, ultimately, she played me for a fool. She wrote:

> I am getting lots of new followers on my page … All these women want to befriend me as I think they believe I have a secret passage to your bedroom. They are all in love with you. It's hilarious, the 66 year old pensioner got to kiss you and they didn't. Speak soon xx.

9

Richard

'Mate, I'm so sorry to have to tell you this, but Richard's gone. He's gone.'

I could hear the emotion in my radio boss Craig Bruce's voice as he told me the news. I'll never forget that phone call. I'll never forget that feeling.

I was on air at Sydney's 2day FM and took the call during a song. I was numb. I desperately wanted it to be a mistake. The numbness was very swiftly replaced by a sharp pain. It's a sharp pain you'll only know if you've lost someone you love to suicide. That sharp pain is now a part of you. And it always will be. I feel it on 6 December every year. I feel it when I see Richard's face or hear his name. And I even feel it now, twelve years later, as I sit down to write this chapter. Always with the same sharpness, the same intensity.

Richard Marsland was an outrageously gifted comedic writer and performer. But more importantly, he was a son, a brother, an uncle, a friend.

My first interaction with Richard was via email. He didn't know me at this point. I only knew him from his hilarious segments on Adelaide's SAFM and I'd managed to track down his email address. I sent him a list of questions about how to get into radio. I wasn't overly confident I'd receive a response but, much to my surprise, he wrote back within an hour.

His reply was insightful, funny and generous. All of the qualities I'd eventually experience firsthand when we became mates. I printed that email and put it on the back of my bedroom door.

It wasn't only the tips Richard shared, it was the fact he'd taken the time. I was just a uni student, a nobody. Richard had nothing to gain from writing back. But he did. And his email was now my link to the radio station I had dreams of one day working at.

It's impossible to do Richard's career justice in a few sentences, but here's a snapshot.

Richard Marsland was a celebrated writer for TV shows hosted by the likes of Rove McManus and Shaun Micallef. You may not know his name but you've probably laughed at his jokes. His star shone most brightly on radio alongside Tony Martin in the brilliant *Get This* program. It was peak Marsland, a wonderful playground for a gloriously absurd comic mind.

The most common word used to describe Richard by people who truly knew him was 'kind'. He oozed generosity of spirit. If I were forced to pick a flaw with Richard, it would be that he was infuriatingly apologetic. Constantly apologising for the most trivial reasons: 'Sorry, man, is my music too loud?'; 'Sorry I'm so late' (when half an hour early); 'Oh, I don't think this script is funny enough, I'm so sorry.' With Richard, it was always funny enough. And then some.

Richard seriously couldn't hurt a fly. In fact, he'd probably apologise to it: 'Hey, I'm so sorry for getting in the way of your flight path to the bin, it won't happen again.'

A year after that initial email I won a competition at SAFM. The prize was a trip to Edinburgh, Scotland, with the entire breakfast show. That's where I really saw Richard's genius at work, and got to know him as a friend.

As well as contributing on-air segments, Richard was the comedy writer for the show. A ball of nervous energy, always concocting something. He'd be pacing frantically with five sketches on the go at once. Farmers Union Iced Coffee in one hand, cigarette in the other. But he'd always find the gold. Then apologise for it running too long.

Now back to that day, and that phone call on 6 December 2008.

I thanked Craig for calling me and told him I had to go home. I don't really remember what happened immediately after the call. I only remember sitting on the floor of the radio studio, sobbing. It was a solo shift so I was completely alone. I was trying to process what had just happened.

I can hear the phone call with Craig so clearly all of these years later, but the minutes and hours after the call are a blur. I have a vague recollection of walking aimlessly around Hyde Park. I sent messages and made phone calls to mutual friends of Richard and me. At this stage I didn't know who knew. I didn't know what to do or where to go. There's no rulebook to prepare you for this. You're in utter shock. In a daze. In an instant, your life has changed forever.

Richard's funeral was on 19 December 2008, at St Ignatius' Church, Norwood, in South Australia. I saw so many familiar faces in the church that day, I felt a sense of belonging, a shared grief. I felt comfortable for the first time since we'd lost him. We were all in it together at the funeral. We all understood. I didn't feel alone like that Saturday in the radio studio.

Marty Sheargold was cracking jokes. Tony Martin delivered a beautifully humorous eulogy. There was even a station wagon handing out icy cold cans of Coke and Farmers Union Iced Coffees. A throwback to the Black Thunders (the promo vehicles used by radio stations). They were being distributed by people in T-shirts that read 'Generic Radio Station'. Richard would've loved that.

It was actually cathartic to laugh again, surrounded by people who loved Richard. We were giving each other permission to laugh again. Richard had given us all so much laughter over the years, so it was a fitting soundtrack to his farewell. As far as funerals go, I felt good. Then I saw Richard's mum and dad.

It was like a sledgehammer to my heart. I can still see them so clearly in my mind as I write this today. Alisson and Peter Marsland weeping, being consoled by family. Preparing to say goodbye to their son. Seeing them in that moment had a profound effect on me. I couldn't look at them for the rest of the service. It hurt too much. It was a grim reminder of the reality of the situation. The finality. We'd all been trying our best to put on a brave face and celebrate Richard with a few laughs. And we were succeeding. But when I caught that glimpse of Alisson and Peter, I saw the faces of two loving parents living a real-life nightmare.

I'd spoken to Richard on the phone roughly a month before and he was the Richard I'd always known. Upbeat, funny, caring, apologetic. So when we lost him, I really struggled to find meaning, to understand what had happened and why it had happened. Only a handful of people in his life knew of his battle. That scared me. And it saddened me.

I often think about how broken Richard must have been to embark on that lonely drive to the Dandenong Ranges, where he was found. I think about the pain he must've been in to decide that that was the option he needed to take.

It's illogical, but you can't help but question yourself. Could I have done more? Did I miss a sign? Those thoughts race in circles around your head at a frantic pace. And they keep you up at night.

Up until that point, I'd never had firsthand experience with depression or suicide. Richard's death affected me deeply. It still does. I have a much stronger understanding of it now. That hasn't come easily, though.

I remember searching for an answer in those weeks and months after his death. Like a reason was going to suddenly appear and it would all make sense. But it doesn't work like that. Richard's dad, Peter, said something that really stuck with me. He said, 'This was not an act of selfishness on his behalf; rather, a loss to his recurring battle with depression. This was a way for Richard to get release from his pain and nothing else.' Those words mean a lot to me, because I know Richard would never intentionally hurt people he cared about. It's still devastatingly sad, and it's still not an answer, but it's something.

I didn't speak about Richard's death publicly for a very long time. I rarely even spoke about it privately. I don't think I knew how to at that stage. Twelve years ago, mental health conversations were nowhere near as prominent as they are now. Particularly among men.

In 2010 I was hosting a breakfast radio show in Perth and our team was planning to devote a morning to mental health conversations. At the time it was something really out of the box.

In the planning meeting, we were given the opportunity to share any personal connections to the subject. I was surprised how much this affected me. I felt uneasy. I wasn't ready to talk about it. There was no pressure, and at that point I don't think some of the team even knew I'd lost a friend to suicide, but my instinct was to withdraw.

I was driving home after work that day and I could feel my eyes getting teary. I pulled over and sat in the car, thinking about the meeting, thinking about the show, thinking about

Richard. I knew what I had to do. I had to face my fear and speak publicly about my loss. I sent an email to the team and told them I had a personal connection to mental health and I'd like to talk about it in the eight o'clock segment the next morning. They were extremely supportive, and didn't ask any questions.

My role on that radio show was to be the fun guy. The silly guy. The lovable fool. The guy who talked about his cats, the guy who sang Justin Bieber parodies, the guy who prank-called half of Perth in 'Sam Mac Gotcha Calls'. (Side note: one time I was recording a prank call pretending to be a police officer when I was interrupted by an actual police officer who arrived at the radio station because he had reports I was impersonating a police officer. The gotcha was on me that day.) So, yes, I was the light relief on the show. That's why the idea of talking openly about something so personal, so tragic, was an enormous step out of my comfort zone.

Throughout that morning's show, all I could think about was how close we were getting to 8 a.m. I was clock watching. Trying desperately to calm my nerves. Reminding myself why opening up was so important.

When 8 a.m. finally arrived, I launched into the segment: 'Guys, I've never spoken publicly about this before, but I've lost a close mate to his battles with mental health.'

I could sense a little bit of shock from my co-hosts. They'd never seen this side of me. I don't think *I'd* ever seen this side of me. I felt extremely vulnerable, frightened. I carried on with the segment but as soon as I said Richard's name, it hit me hard. A wave of emotion. Suddenly it wasn't a radio segment, it wasn't about the thousands of people listening in – it was about Richard.

I'd spent hours the night before thinking about what I wanted to say. I rarely script or prepare anything to that degree. Just ask The Human Emoji. But it was so important that I did Richard justice. I'd asked Alisson and Peter for permission to talk about him, which they had very kindly granted. I didn't know a lot about mental health back then, so I was also terrified of saying the wrong thing. That stigma still exists. People who say nothing in fear of saying the wrong thing. Please say something.

I continued with the segment: 'I just wish I'd known what Richard was going through. I wish I could've done more. I wish I had a chance to tell him how loved he was and that we could've helped him get through this.'

By this point, I was really struggling. My breathing was audible and very stilted. The tone of my voice was wavering up and down. My co-hosts had to fill the gaps while I tried to regain my composure. It was a mess. I was a mess. But I had to keep going. It wasn't about me.

Thank goodness I had prepared those notes. They gave me a focus. The average segment length on our show was three to four minutes. This went for almost ten. By the end I couldn't even look at my co-hosts. I remember staring at the microphone. Seeing my own tears fall onto it.

But I made it to the end. I said everything I wanted to say. After the segment the content director, Mickey Maher, also in tears, gave me an enormous hug. He knew how difficult that was for me. He said he was extremely proud of me for pushing through and saying what I wanted to say. He said it would've made Richard proud too.

I didn't know it at the time, but it would turn out to be a pivotal moment in my life. It was the moment I showed myself that I could do it. I could talk openly about mental health and the loss of a friend. Sure, it wasn't smooth, and it was, at times, uncomfortably raw. But that's authenticity. That's being a human. And I'm not ashamed of that. Nor should anyone else be.

I don't subscribe to that 'men shouldn't cry' bullshit that some people do. Of course men should cry. It makes you more of a man to cry, or to speak openly and show your truth.

If I can't share deeply personal emotions, if I can't show vulnerability, then it would be hypocritical of me to expect others to. That's the point. That's why I did it. I had to practise what I was preaching, and speak up even though it was really bloody hard.

The following weekend I was at Subiaco Stadium. I worked there for two seasons as ground announcer for the Fremantle Dockers. I was minding my own business, watching the game, when a young lad approached me. He would've been early twenties. I don't even remember his name. But I remember very clearly what he said to me.

'Hey, Sam,' he said, 'I was listening to your radio segment on mental health and it came just when I needed it. I've been through a really tough break-up. And I'm having some family problems. And I've just been feeling really lost. I've been having some pretty dark thoughts. But when you spoke about your mate, it woke something up in me. It made me realise the pain left behind. So I checked out Beyond Blue like you suggested, and I spoke to my parents. They've been amazing and are booking some counselling for me. So I just wanted to say thanks from the bottom of my heart for what you did. I know it wasn't easy for you.'

That moment right there. That one-minute conversation with a guy whose name I can't even remember. It instantly filled my soul with pride. It was incredibly humbling to know that my words and my experience had played a role in guiding someone, a complete stranger, in the right direction. It gave me a sense of purpose I'd never felt before. It was crystal clear from that day forwards that my mission was to use my platform to be a vocal supporter of mental health conversations, particularly among men.

In 2016, my first year on *Sunrise*, we were scheduled to do a morning of live crosses for R U OK? Day. I decided this would be the right moment for me to share my personal connection to mental health with the *Sunrise* viewers.

I touched base with Alisson Marsland first to make sure she was comfortable with me talking about Richard on TV. She was as supportive as ever.

I then arranged with The Human Emoji to have some nice photos of Richard ready to accompany the live cross. I can't express how important it is to me that I do a great job with these pieces. They mean more to me than any other segment. I want to make the Marslands proud, and I want to do Richard justice.

The entire experience was eerily similar to the first time I spoke about Richard on radio in Perth. It was on my mind constantly in the lead-up. I felt the same nerves. I wasn't entirely present during the rest of the show; my focus was on that one moment. I even did it in the same eight o'clock timeslot. But this time I didn't break down.

It was obviously still a big step out of my comfort zone, particularly as I was the new guy on the show and I hadn't shown this kind of vulnerability to the *Sunrise* audience yet. But I said everything I wanted to say and I felt much more in control this time.

The Human Emoji made a point of saying how proud he was of me for doing it. It meant a lot to have his backing, both as a friend and as a producer. I know that he truly cares, he's a good person (they can be surprisingly rare in TV), and we both felt such a sense of satisfaction after contributing something truly meaningful to the show. And, most importantly, the Marslands were happy.

Doing the segment on TV was quite different to doing it on radio. This time people could see Richard. People could see my face. My expressions. My eyes reddening. From my perspective, there's nowhere to hide. Those TV lights are bright and unforgiving. You really are putting your vulnerability on the line for all to see. But that's why it connects. And it's not about me. I kept reminding myself of that when it got tough.

The response was instant and immense. I might have slightly underestimated the reach of *Sunrise*. The volume of messages and comments that came through was extraordinary. My Facebook, Twitter and Instagram were bombarded. I remember looking at my phone minutes after the segment and seeing notification after notification. It was nonstop.

The majority of the messages were from people commending me for speaking so openly about such a challenging and confronting subject. What surprised me was how willing people were to share their own experiences with mental health. It doesn't get much more personal than that. It was almost as if they were looking for someone to talk to, and my segment had given them the green light. I love that.

Some messages definitely felt like a cry for help. I take all feedback in this area very, very seriously. I make a point of trying to reply to every single message. And as quickly as I can. This is not always realistic. But I try.

It's so important to me that people feel seen. That they feel heard. That it's a positive experience. Because I know for a fact, for some of these people, I am the first person they've reached out to. Often people are too ashamed or too embarrassed to reach out to a loved one.

Certain messages stand out. I had one lady, who will remain anonymous, write to me essentially saying she couldn't go on anymore. Her depression was defeating her. She told me she felt like such a failure in every aspect of her life and that she'd be doing everyone a favour by ending her life. The biggest alarm bell in this message to me was that she even went into detail about how she was planning to kill herself.

The message had a dramatic impact on me. They don't come much heavier. I spoke to my contact at R U OK? and responded as quickly as I could. It obviously felt very urgent. In my response I made sure she knew I was proud of her for sharing with me. I wanted to make it a positive interaction. Or she might not ever reach out to anyone again.

I decided to respond in a personal manner. I told her about my connection to mental health. I told her about Richard, and how heartbreaking his death was and is for his loved ones. I told her about his funeral. I told her about how much his friends and family would give just to be able to hug him again. I ensured her that there is another path, and that she can do it.

I pointed out that I wasn't a psychiatrist or a professional counsellor. I couldn't be that on-call support network. But I gently encouraged her to tell a loved one in her life, and to have a look at some of the incredible support networks out there. And that was where our correspondence ended.

One year later, on R U OK? Day, after almost a year without contact, she wrote this direct message to me on Facebook:

Hi Sam. I know you get lots of messages, and probably too many to read. But last year, you helped me not hang myself. I kept thinking about what you said about your friend and how it affects everyone left behind. So I built up the courage to tell my husband and I got help from there.

That message stopped me in my tracks. I read it again. And again. I went for a walk to digest it. I had that same feeling I had after chatting to the young guy at the footy in Perth. A lifting of the soul. I often hear people talk about their purpose. Or doing what they're on this earth to do. That's how I feel in these moments.

I'm realistic – I know I can't help everyone. But I can use my platform and help someone. And that's why it's worth it, and that's why I'll keep chipping away.

Being an ambassador for mental health conversations with R U OK? Day is one of the most rewarding things I do. This chapter has been the most difficult one to write (and I'm not even finished yet) but I know in my gut it's the most important one (sorry, Coco).

On R U OK? Day in 2020 I revealed a little challenge I'd set myself. I'd decided to wear my yellow R U OK? Day wristband every single day for an entire year. No matter where I was or what I was doing, I had the wristband on. Initially it was to keep me in tune for mental health conversations, but I eventually found it to be a great little symbolic reminder that you never really know what someone else is going through, whether it's a workmate you sit near or even a complete stranger.

I think we can all do better in this space. A little extra kindness and emotional awareness can make a world of difference to someone in a dark place. And before you nickname me 'stinky wristband boi', no, it wasn't the same wristband every day. I made a point of changing the wristband every time I changed my sheets. So, twice a year.

As I touched on earlier, when you lose a friend to suicide, you seek answers. You search for meaning and you try to piece it together to make some sort of sense. Like a jigsaw puzzle. That's just what the human brain does. Sadly, it's not a jigsaw puzzle. Or perhaps it is, but there are multiple pieces missing. So, in an attempt to gain a better understanding, I decided to interview my friend Sez.

Sez is a beautiful, compassionate, funny, intelligent woman in her thirties. On the surface, her life was grand. But earlier this year Sez attempted suicide. I'm so grateful that it was a failed attempt, because I know how much she has to bring to the world, and I love seeing her flourish in recovery.

Sez is the closest connection I have to someone who knows what it feels like to be suicidal. She very kindly agreed to answer a couple of questions that I think will give all of us a better understanding of that headspace.

Did you think about suicide a lot? Or was it more of a sharp response to something?

'Yes, I thought about suicide possibly daily. And I still have those thoughts, perhaps not daily, however every now and then the thoughts creep in. I've always known how I would do it. I wanted it to be as painless as possible.'

When you're in that state, at your absolute lowest, can you still think about your loved ones and what it would do to them?

'This is a complex one. It's hard to explain to someone who has never felt the depth of emotional pain that I, or others, have felt. Imagine someone that is in extreme, devastating pain due to a brain tumour – though instead of a visible, tangible mass growing inside their head, it's a culmination of emotional pain, trauma etc. ... That pain extends to their heart, their stomach. Everything aches and you just want to be free of it. We don't judge the terminally ill cancer patient for wanting their pain to end but for a mentally ill person, they can be labelled as selfish, weak ... Something the people who are left behind need to understand is that *it's not about them*. They weren't living the life the person who chose to leave was living, they were *never* experiencing their mental landscape.

'I know this because when I was broken, at my lowest point, my soul was done. When it came down to it, there was nothing anyone could have said or done. I'd decided the night before, I went to bed knowing what the next day was for, and that's all there was to it. I'd disconnected. I'm in no way advocating suicide and I agree that as a collective community we can do more. I'm simply saying people who are left behind shouldn't punish or admonish themselves. The world is already a hard place to live in and mental illness doesn't make it any easier.'

Finally, do you have advice for people reading this who don't have mental illness?
'Be a good person.

Be kind to strangers.

Try not to take things personally.

Learn how to communicate effectively.

Uncover what your generational traumas are so you don't pass them onto your children.'

I took so much from those responses. I hope you did too. Her brain tumour analogy really opened me up to a new way of looking at mental health battles. It was blunt and powerful. An important reminder that we can't presume to know or understand someone's internal suffering. I'd also recommend reading her advice for people without mental illness a couple of times. There are some very simple, yet important reminders in there for all of us.

I really admire Sez's bravery and generosity in sharing such personal insights to help others. When I initially approached her, she said she'd do it on the condition she could give me the 'real answers, not the Disney answers'. That she did. Love and respect to you, Sez – I'm proud of you.

One of the most common questions I get asked online and in person when I discuss mental health is whether or not I'm okay myself. I appreciate the concern. And I'm pleased to say that I am okay. My mental health is consistently strong. I would never flippantly undermine the seriousness of depression, anxiety or any form of mental health battle. Of course, I have good days and bad days. We all do. And that's totally cool. And normal.

I stay on top of my mental health by making balance a priority. My job and the travel and pressure that come with it can be relentless. I need to make room for the downtime. I lounge around and watch Netflix. I listen to meditation and manifestation podcasts. I unwind with friends. And I always make time to have a strum on the guitar (or form my own superband with a famous TV vet – more on that later). They're the techniques that work for me.

On a recent work trip to the Barossa Valley in Adelaide, I managed to catch up with Alisson and Peter Marsland. I care so deeply for them. And I feel a unique affinity with them. I guess it's comforting to have a tangible link to Richard. I didn't spend a lot of time with them when Richard was alive. But I chat regularly to Alisson on Facebook and have done ever since we lost Richard. I see them as extended family. I have to make sure they're okay. It's hard to describe.

We sat down and had a few drinks. We shared story after story about Richard. They're so incredibly proud of him, and I was delighted to see how comfortable they were talking about him. Like any parent would be. I learnt things about Richard I never knew. Like how talented he was with drawings and stories from a very young age. The Marslands told me of the wine they'd created in Richard's honour, called Richard's Run. The label on the bottle is a bird Richard hand-drew when he was a youngster. So special.

I know it's probably frowned upon in the literary world to promote a website or a product in a book, but it's my book and I'll do what I want (as long as my publisher, Sophie, approves obviously). I'd like to welcome you all to order a bottle from the Marslands and raise a toast to Richard via www.marsiewines.com Tell them Sam sent you.

When I saw the Marslands, of course there were tears. Of course there were difficult pauses and sorrowful sighs.

Of course we just wished Richard could've been there with us. But that wasn't meant to be. And besides, we wouldn't have got through those amazing stories as he would've been constantly apologising for it all being about him.

Towards the end of the catch-up, much like at the funeral, the reality of the situation hit me. I don't know why that always happens to me. Alisson was telling another Richard story. A funny one. They're all funny ones. She was laughing hysterically. It was wonderful. But the sense of loss was still there. I could feel it. Lingering. I love that more than a decade on, Richard still brings that joy to her face. But I know behind the smile, behind those eyes, Alisson is

a mum who would give anything to be able to hug her little boy again, and tell him she loves him.

As we were saying our goodbyes with a few long hugs, Alisson said something that hit me for six. She said, 'Your parents must be so proud of you, Sam. I know I am. We always see a little bit of Richard in you. The same wonderful personality and sense of fun, but a genuineness to all of the people you meet.'

That's the highest compliment I've ever been given. From someone I truly admire. It still gives me shivers and fills me with pride.

I'd like to finish this chapter by encouraging you to look out for your friends and loved ones. Nothing major. Nothing overly dramatic. Just be in tune with any changes or challenges they may be facing. Do everything you can to provide a safe space for them to talk. And if you're going through mental health challenges yourself, please believe me when I say there is *always* someone to talk to. Whether it's personal or professional. There is always help, and you are loved.

This book is dedicated to the generosity of spirit and fun of Richard Kemble Marsland. Sorry, mate.

10

Naked

'Okay, guys, you're on in one minute!'

I'm backstage at Sydney's Enmore Theatre about to get completely naked in front of a thousand strangers and 1.5 million TV viewers. Even though I've been mentally and physically preparing myself for this moment for six weeks, it's become very real when the stage manager gives us that one-minute warning. I'm pacing nervously. Breathing heavily. Sweating profusely. A green exit door light flickers in the corner of my eyesight. I genuinely weigh up what the repercussions would be if I beelined for the door and jumped in the next available Uber.

'*The Real Full Monty* on stage in ten seconds, please, gentlemen.'

Right now you're probably wondering the same thing I was wondering: *Why on earth did he say yes to this?*

Rewind the clock a few months and I'm in New Zealand for *Sunrise*. I was on an afternoon walk when I received a call from my manager, Melissa Harvey. I noticed an unusually menacing tone in her voice.

'We've had a very interesting proposal come through, Sam,' she said. 'How do you feel about getting your gear off?'

This will shock you, but I'm not exactly inundated with requests to take my clothes off. In my professional or private life, sadly.

'I'm all for taking risks, Mel, but I'm probably gonna need more information,' I said.

Melissa proceeded to pitch the concept for an upcoming prime-time TV special called *The Real Full Monty*. Eight male celebrities would bare all in a choreographed strip routine to raise awareness for men's health. Mel explained how successful the show – inspired by the smash-hit movie *The Full Monty* – had been in the UK and how a vehicle like this would be an excellent opportunity to show the audience a different part of me. Yeah, a different part of me all right! A part of me that ordinarily if shown to an audience would land me in the back of a divvy van.

Despite her best efforts to sell the concept and the very worthy cause attached to it, all I was hearing on that call was 'penis, penis, penis, penis, penis'.

(Side note: you know how websites and magazines use little excerpts from books to promote them? I would find it highly amusing if the only quote they used from mine was that piece of literary genius.)

That's right: I wasn't convinced. Even though I do occasionally push the envelope on *Sunrise*, I'm quite protective of the fact that it's a family show. Mums and dads often write to me on social media with photos and videos of their kids interacting with my content. It's pretty cool. So I'm well aware of who's watching and I put a lot of effort into keeping things family friendly. (I'm also well aware of the fact I've just contradicted myself by using the word penis multiple times in one sentence.)

After a fifteen-minute discussion, my response was no. It just felt a bit smutty for my liking and, if I'm honest, the idea of getting completely naked in front of cameras, colleagues and strangers felt like a horrific nightmare slash potential court case.

Mel informed the production company of my decision and the reasons behind it. The executive producer of the show then asked if he could speak to me directly. I was more than happy to take the call.

'Look,' he said, 'I understand why you said no. We totally get the *Sunrise* thing. But I just want you to hear me out and watch a five-minute promo video of the UK version.'

His pitch was impressive, with much more focus on *why* we were doing it. He was extremely passionate about raising awareness for men's health, and passion is contagious.

I watched the video and it was some of the most powerful TV I'd seen in a long time. Yes, there was nudity, but it was delivered in a playful, cheeky fashion. Nudity was the hook to attract attention and viewers to the show. But the focus was on communicating important information about men's health. The show included interviews with prostate and testicular cancer survivors. We heard from their families. We saw big burly men breaking down and telling us that if they hadn't gone to the doctor to get tested, they may not have been alive to see their daughter get married.

I was in – it was too important not to do it. I spoke to Mel and we informed them I was now a yes. Damn that executive producer for being so good at his job!

I've found that, particularly in this role, when I do put myself out of my comfort zone, 99 per cent of the time I'm glad I did it. The exception was bungee jumping ...

As I mentioned earlier, I had to bungee jump in 2016 on my very first day as the *Sunrise* weatherman. It must've been payback for going too hard in contract negotiations. So much for easing me into the gig.

Sean had sounded me out ahead of time on what I was really uncomfortable doing and foolishly I had said, 'I don't mind, mate, as long as it's not jumping out of a plane,' but I made no mention of bungee jumping! So he had me on a technicality.

It's 5.40 a.m. in Logan, Queensland. I'm wearing a blindfold and all I know at the time is that I'm somewhere close to Brisbane. Kochie and Sam welcome me to the show and instruct me to remove my blindfold. I take it off and see a mini racetrack.

'Cool, I love go-karting,' I say.

They tell me to turn around. I do so and see an enormous black-and-white sign with one word on it: 'Bungee!' I am petrified. Never in a million years would I bungee jump willingly. The pay-off just doesn't outweigh the risk and trauma. What *is* the pay-off? I think it's just the realisation and euphoria that the rope worked and you didn't die. But what did you achieve? You just didn't die! Why put yourself through that? I can get adrenaline in other ways. Like dressing my cat up in a tutu and cat glasses from Japan.

So I'm standing on the bungee ledge reassessing my career and life decisions. I am scheduled to jump in our prime-time cross at 8 a.m. But the team want me up there for the two crosses prior to build up the hype. That means an excruciating hour standing up there alone, waiting.

My strategy is simple: *whatever you do, just don't look down.* This is particularly tough as I really want to shoot a few death stares at The Human Emoji.

I am genuinely scared – as in, stomach-churningly scared. And the audience, I think, can feel my pain. That is a good thing. This is my first strong connection with the *Sunrise* viewers, and I imagine many of them would be feeling exactly the same if they were about to bungee jump. Authenticity stands out on TV because it's surprisingly rare. The viewers also know that they don't have to go through with the jump, because I'm about to do it for them.

While you're standing on that ledge, every single part of your body and brain is telling you not to move forwards. It's human instinct. That's how we're brought up. To stay safe. Only you can make that decision, and that leap, to go against everything you've ever learnt.

The one thing working in my favour – and ultimately the thing that helps me get through it – is my earpiece. That tiny crackly earpiece means I can hear the hosts in the studio. It is enough to take my mind elsewhere as I prepare to jump.

Kochie and Sam start the countdown: 'Five, four, three, two, one – bungeeeeeee!'

Your body moves in slow motion, as if to say, 'Are you sure, bro?'

There was an intense internal struggle happening as I listened to that countdown. On the one hand I was dealing with fear, knowing I'm about to do something I really don't want to do. On the other hand, I'm an entertainer at heart. I live to entertain. It pushes me to do things I otherwise wouldn't. I also have an ego and I don't want my first day to be a failure.

I jump.

'Arrrrrrggggggghhhhhhhh ... arrrrrrgggggggghhhhhh ... I am not extreeeeeeeeme ... arrrrrgggggghhhhhhh ... I love you, Mum ... I love you, Dad ... arrrrrrrggggghhhhhhhh ... You sent Edwina to a cotton farm on her first day!'

Clearly, I'm not at my most eloquent when flying through the air attached by my legs to a piece of rope. I am proud, however, that even while upside down, I still managed to highlight the double standards between my first day and my predecessor Edwina Bartholomew's first day on the job.

Relief. Pure relief. That's what I felt once it was over. Perhaps a hint of pride for conquering a fear. But to everyone asking if I enjoyed the adrenaline rush or wanted to do it again: absolutely not. I would rather get completely nude in front of the nation ... Oh yes, where were we?

The Real Full Monty was a different kind of ledge, but I still had instincts telling me it was an enormous jump, and that something could go dramatically and potentially career-endingly wrong.

I found the best way to counteract these fears was to replace them with reminders of the cause and how this crazy idea could genuinely save lives. The mission of the show was to encourage men to get checked for testicular and prostate cancer. An extremely worthy mission. So many men, particularly older men, will only agree to visit a doctor to have a limb reattached. Even then, they'd probably have a crack at it themselves first via a DIY YouTube tutorial.

I knew this show was also the perfect platform to encourage men to speak up about their mental health. This desire was coming from a very real place for me because of what happened to my friend Richard Marsland. I had agreed to sign on with the proviso that some of my air time would be dedicated to destigmatising mental health conversations, particularly among men. It meant the world to me that the producers delivered on that promise. Anyway, back to the nudity.

Nothing motivates you to eat and train properly more than the knowledge that you're about to perform a striptease for the nation. The show was more than just a striptease though – as well as interviews with cancer survivors, it documented the behind-the-scenes work we did to get ready. This meant that filming was a six-week commitment of three or four days a week, and I was also working on *Sunrise* at the time so these were long days. Cameras followed us every poorly choreographed step of the way in the build-up to the big night. They captured us meeting our fellow celebrities, learning the dance moves, getting in shape, getting our outfits and generally bonding through the process. The audience would ultimately see us transform from a group of amateur strippers to ... well, a slightly more cohesive group of amateur strippers.

On a few occasions I was interstate with *Sunrise*, so I'd do the show then get on the 9.30 a.m. flight back to Sydney, work a full day filming with *The Real Full Monty*, then fly back to Toowoomba or wherever I was for the next day's show. It was particularly gruelling. On top of that, I was training every day.

Two of my great mates are qualified personal trainers: Chris Coates in Perth and Simon Mitchell in Adelaide. They both asked me not to mention their names in the book as being associated with my naked body is apparently bad for business. Sorry, gents!

Chris and Simon staged a complete intervention on my diet. I remember reading the eating plan and in unnecessarily large red text it said, 'YOU ARE OFFICIALLY BANNED

FROM EATING CARBS FOR SIX WEEKS.' I began to process what that meant. Bread, gone. Pasta, gone. Beer, gone. Oh, the inhumanity! These two alleged friends of mine had done a reverse Marie Kondo. They'd savagely thrown out all of the things in my life that sparked joy!

On day one of filming we were introduced to our fellow celebrities. Kris Smith, former rugby league star and actual male model. Great! Matt Cooper, former rugby league star and underwear model. Wonderful! Jett Kenny, ironman slash model. Are you kidding me? Surely the producers were having a laugh. I was pitched a show starring everyday blokes getting their gear off for a good cause. Now I discover I'll be getting naked next to an ironman slash model? Ironman slash model sounds like a three-word Tinder bio that no one would swipe right on because it's obviously fake.

I'm a straight man, but even I was struck by Jett's beauty. He looked like he was designed by a computer program. Piercing blue eyes, check. Flowing blond locks, check. Eight pack of abs, check. Not only did he have bonus abs, he even had a bonus T in his name … And that's absolutely a flex to other inferior Jets out there struggling through life with just the one T.

I hate to bang on about Jett Kenny, but he's one of those people who legitimately stops traffic. The traffic is either stopping to marvel at him and take photos, or it's stopping because it collided with him and is now ricocheting off his thick pecs.

Later that day I did some research and discovered that he wasn't created by a computer program – even better, he was created by a breeding program between two former Olympians! Okay, I made the breeding program bit up, but his parents are both sporting icons, former Olympians Lisa Curry and Grant Kenny. Incredible! And do you know the part that I found most offensive about this whole Jett Kenny thing? It's that he's actually a really lovely guy. Well, a really lovely guy for an ironman slash model. Eyeroll emoji.

Making up the numbers alongside me in our male strip squad were commentator Brian 'BT' Taylor, AFL player Campbell Brown, actor Shane Jacobson and radio host Brendan 'Jonesy' Jones.

The man entrusted with teaching us how to strip and dance simultaneously was Todd McKenney. Some of you will know Todd as the original Peter Allen in *The Boy from Oz*. Others will know him as the scathing judge on *Dancing with the Stars*. For a novice dancer like myself, I had a feeling this was not going to be a gentle education.

I've never been afraid to try new things on TV; it's a big part of what I do on *Sunrise*. I've always had the mantra that from a TV perspective, 'failure is funny'. Thankfully failure comes quite naturally to me. Just ask any of my ex-girlfriends.

So even though I knew nothing about dancing, me trying something and spectacularly failing is often a better result than me trying something and nailing it – because who wants to watch a guy who's good at everything? It would become boring. You could even start to dislike the guy. It'd be like an ironman who's also good at modelling. Infuriating, right? Okay, I'll stop. Sorry, Jett.

Sunrise viewers have watched me struggle to change a tyre, struggle to learn how to knit, struggle to walk in heels and, most commonly of all, struggle to share any convincing knowledge of the weather. Failure is funny. And it can be very endearing. By the end of our first choreography lesson, however, I'd learnt that Todd McKenney may disagree with my failure-is-funny mantra. He had no hesitation instructing us to repeat the same dance move seventeen times in a row until we got it right. You could really see how he got to the top of his game. He was like a smiling assassin. A flamboyant footy coach.

One day at rehearsals I couldn't execute a particular step and it was really getting to me. So I asked Todd to help me learn it. He patted me on the back and very casually said, 'Don't worry, mate, you've got nothing to worry about – we'll have the hotties with the rigs up the front, and you'll be hidden at the back.' Ouch. Thanks for the inspirational pep talk, coach.

In the back of my mind throughout the six weeks of filming was the apprehension and lingering fear of eventually showing my nude self to Australia. I don't have body dysmorphia, but I'm also not one of those 'nudie run' or 'shower with the boys' kind of guys. You'll never find me at the beach in Speedos. In fact, I often wear a T-shirt and legionnaire's hat at the beach to protect my fair skin and freckles. (Can't wait for the avalanche of DMs from single ladies after that sentence.) It just makes sense to cover up and be sun smart. Shout-out to Mum and Dad for my Irish heritage! My alleged friend Matt Doran once described my complexion as 'translucent'. And some cameramen have even been known to conduct their pre-shoot 'white balance' on my skin. That joke will make sense to 0.4 per cent of readers, but it's staying in.

So imagine my surprise when, in the days leading up to the performance, the producers took us on a group excursion to Beach Street Tanning. We were handed a questionnaire about the level of tan we desired. The various tans had names like Subtle Glow and Beach Babe. Jules, who was helping with my tan, asked me when the last time I had a spray tan was. 'In 2011 for a radio stunt,' was my reply. I'm just not a spray-tan kind of guy.

Next, Jules asked how I would describe my natural complexion. I told her I'd describe it as 'whiter than a

Pauline Hanson rally'. We both agreed that Subtle Glow was the tan for me.

We were instructed to go completely nude in the tanning booth, otherwise one part of our body would be noticeably paler than the rest. I didn't know what Jules's annual salary was but I was almost certain she was not paid enough to be subjected to this. I could see the pain in her eyes when she learnt she'd be tanning me and not ironman slash model Jett Kenny.

Fifteen minutes later I emerged from the booth. I remember my last words to the group before going in: 'Just make sure it's not anything crazy because I'm still on air this week with *Sunrise*.' Well, as I checked the mirror after the tan, it quickly became apparent that there'd been a 'miscommunication'. And by 'miscommunication' I mean 'absolute stitch-up by evil producers'.

I did not emerge with the Subtle Glow we'd agreed on; instead, I was now sporting a tan called Chocolate Mousse. Wow. Judging by the bursts of laughter echoing through the salon, more people were in on this than I was aware. I genuinely looked like a different person. *Sunrise* viewers would be waking up tomorrow thinking, *Umm, why is Pete Evans doing the weather?*

Not long after, the big day I'd been dreading for six weeks finally arrived. The mood was eerily quiet on our minibus drive to Sydney's Enmore Theatre. Showtime was just hours away and you could feel the nerves.

We had one final walk on the stage while the theatre was still empty. Shane and Todd presented us with our custom-made G-strings. That's a sentence I never thought would appear in my first book.

The G-strings were in glittering showbiz red, with buttons and velcro either side for swift removal. It was quite a surreal experience being handed a G-string by another man and being told to try it on and see how it feels.

Next minute I'm in a change room with Kris Smith – of course it was Kris Smith. Of all of the physiques I could possibly be next to when I needed that final confidence boost, it's rugby star slash male model Kris Smith. Why couldn't it have been BT?

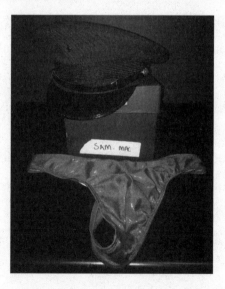

I tried on the G-string and, as the material wedged between my butt cheeks, I had a new level of respect for women.

(Side note: I've just realised that parts of this chapter could push my book into the lucrative erotic non-fiction genre. Talk to me, Hachette.)

My G-string fit fine. I think. I can't say I enjoyed feeling the gentle cotton on my bottom, but it was manageable. It was slightly less manageable at the front, where the fit was particularly snug. So much so that I had to make an important storage decision. This might be too much information – too late now – but I decided to go with what I call 'The Beyoncé Technique' and stored it 'to the left, to the left'.

It turned out most of the guys had 'shaved down' – as in, down there. I was not privy to this strategy. Should I follow their lead? At times like this you need someone you can turn to, someone respected globally for their philosophical pearls of wisdom. Of course, I speak of Kris Smith, who told me, 'If you trim the hedge, it makes the tree look bigger, son.' I was sold. I decided on a slight tidy-up. Just a neat trim. Besides, time was of the essence, and I didn't think a Jim's Mowing franchisee would've been able to do a call-out before showtime.

We could hear the crowd entering the theatre. Our energy levels lifted. T minus thirty minutes. I was called to the dressing room for something called 'body make-up'. It was essentially two ladies covering up any marks and vigorously rubbing oil all over your body. I love body make-up.

I asked them if they could help accentuate my ab – singular. All of my training and dieting had paid off. I honestly did have the outline of an ab – singular. A great set of ab.

On a serious note: I felt like I was in career-best shape. I'd really applied myself. I remember being very stressed about the fact I was going to get naked on stage and on camera, but I was equally stressed about letting Todd McKenney down with my chore' (that's short for choreography, you can only say it once you're a legit dancer, sorry).

With just fifteen minutes until our final call, we met a young man named Michael. He shared his incredible story with the group. Michael was only in his early thirties, yet he had survived testicular cancer twice. It gave me shivers. The room fell silent. We were hanging on every word from this very impressive man. After five powerful minutes he finished by saying how proud he was of us for putting our bodies on the line to encourage more men to pay attention to their health. He started a clap, we all joined in, and I don't think I'd ever been more pumped up in my life.

By this stage, we started to hear the crowd. It was rowdy. Ninety-nine per cent female. Over a thousand people were crammed into that audience. They informed us the show was a sellout – which was slightly misleading as the tickets were free.

Again, this is probably too much information (I think that ship has sailed), but a big topic of conversation on the day was about giving ourselves a little 'gee-up' just before going on. You know, getting some blood flowing. So as to give the best account of ourselves. This is my main recollection of the minutes before going on. Some closed their eyes and pictured inspiration in an almost meditative state. Others took private calls from their wives. I was single, so I had a quick scan of J-Lo's Instagram. What? I'm just a passionate supporter of Latino pop. Feeling inspired.

'Ladies and gentlemen, please welcome, *The Real Full Monty*!'

The curtains were drawn back. The song we'd heard almost a thousand times over the past six weeks, 'You Can Leave Your Hat On', blasted out of the speakers. But this time it was the real deal. The crowd was so loud – and we could see them. I felt such a buzz. I was loving the showmanship of the performance. Smiling, winking, absolutely working that crowd into a frenzy.

The song was flying by so fast, but timing was everything and we had a job to do. And much like Eminem in *8 Mile*, we only had one opportunity, we only had one shot. Although while Eminem needed to lose himself in the moment, we were about to lose our pants in the moment.

The final move of the routine was supposed to be the group throwing our hats into the air. The big reveal.

The moment arrived, Joe Cocker's voice booming through the Enmore Theatre that we could leave our hats on. We vigorously removed our hats from our groins. Freedom! Stark naked. The culmination of six weeks of intense build-up. It was bizarrely exhilarating.

The blinder lights and pyrotechnics provided a much-needed distraction. We'd agreed to let it all hang out for three seconds before covering up and getting off stage. I only realised after the fact that I was the only one who didn't throw the hat! Even in an indoor strip routine, I'm still sun smart. And my three seconds was actually closer to 1.4 seconds, despite it feeling like a solid month.

The crowd went berserk. We'd done it. It was deafening, and the response from the crowd felt like we were riding a wave of love.

Backstage it was all high-fives and bum taps. Beers were flowing. Body parts were dangling. It was like the world's most homoerotic football change room.

We then put our robes on and headed back onstage for a Q&A – something I think all strippers should consider doing. The crowd were wonderfully supportive. I told them about my tan and how they should be thankful that it was me who said yes to the show and not Kochie.

Jett told everyone that the worst part was ten seconds before the big reveal when he accidentally made eye contact with his sister in the front row. Who sits in the front row to watch a sibling get naked? Well, I guess not everybody's sibling is an ironman slash model.

The show was a critical and ratings success. I'm forever grateful to Sonya Wilkes and Brad Gustafson, who not only cast me but also delivered an end product that delicately balanced nudity and fun with an extremely important message. The message was never tokenistic.

I had twenty friends over – mainly women, surprisingly enough – for a viewing party at my house on the night it went to air. It was an emotional rollercoaster. One minute they were crying, the next minute they were cheering like it was a sporting event and telling us to 'take it off'.

In the days after the show went to air I was inundated with hundreds of messages commending our bravery. Countless examples of women telling us they watched with their dad, or brother or partner, and how the show had persuaded many of them to finally book in at the doctor for a check-up. This made me so happy.

But there was one message that struck a chord with me like no other. I received it on Facebook a week after the show had aired. The woman was comfortable with me sharing it, but wanted to remain anonymous.

Hey Sam, my eldest son has been suffering bad depression for a while but in recent months it has intensified due to job loss and the loss of his girlfriend. He kept it quiet because he 'didn't want to worry anyone'. Around the time you did *The Real Full Monty* he was suicidal and unbeknownst to us had a failed attempt at an overdose. The morning after the show, we were discussing the story you shared of the friend you lost to suicide. He immediately broke down, cried into my shoulder, and told me about what had happened with his attempt. We talked about his headspace and went to the Dr for assessment. He got meds and fast tracked to see a clinical psychologist. He's still not 100% but I can now support him properly as he recovers. I can't say thank you enough mate, you saved my son's life, well and truly. I owe you everything. You don't even know us but you touched us with the best gift any human on this earth could give and I will forever be in your debt. Sorry for the babble, but I wanted you to know. x

I had a physical reaction to those words. I felt them. I cried. And I'm crying now as I revisit this moment. My words will never be able to truly express what that message means to me. It vindicated my involvement with the show and my decisions times a million. If that woman is reading this, thank you.

The other great achievement to come out of this project was revealed in a chat with my manager, Melissa Harvey, who called me one day to say, 'Congratulations, Sam, you're now the only client on our books who we have a G-string measurement for.' #Proud.

Since the show, I've had a number of people ask me how I managed to go through with that final part of the striptease. The reveal. I guess my advice would be very similar to my advice for bungee jumping: whatever you do, don't look down!

11

Hacked

'Hey man, what's going on with your Facebook?'

That was the text message I received from a friend on the evening of 4 November 2019.

I remember being confused by the question. I hadn't been on Facebook all day.

Beep beep. Another message: 'Sam, are you all good?'

Something was obviously going down, and I had no idea what it was.

Seconds later, *beep beep*, yet another text message: 'Get onto your Facebook ASAP, mate, I think you've been hacked.'

I opened my Facebook page and couldn't believe what I saw. All of the text had been changed to Arabic. And my profile picture had been updated to a group of men celebrating while holding an ISIS flag. Something tells me they weren't celebrating a sporting event.

Time stood still as I tried to comprehend how and why this was happening. I began to panic.

Now, I do some pretty out-there things on social media, but it's safe to say changing my profile picture to an ISIS flag is not an idea I'd ever consider. And it's definitely something marketing experts would refer to as being 'off brand'.

The text messages were now flooding in. I didn't know what to do. I was panicking.

Before I could take any action I noticed my Facebook page was shutting down and effectively locking me out of my own page. I frantically tried to log back in, but was informed I now had the incorrect password.

I tried my Instagram but was locked out of that account as well. Twitter, same deal.

In an act of desperation I thought I could go via my email and set up new passwords. I entered the login details for my email, and my heart sank as I read the words 'Your password has been changed'. I was now blocked from all of my accounts.

People were texting me screenshots of the content. It wasn't pretty. My Twitter account was tweeting photos of people smoking enormous doobies. Again, slightly off brand.

My Facebook page was now posting a new ISIS flag photo every ten minutes. At least there was some brand consistency there.

On a serious note, I was terrified. I felt completely helpless. I didn't know if this was a targeted personal attack on me, or just a random attack on my account because I had a lot of followers.

My manager, Melissa Harvey, and Vanessa Till from Seven publicity were doing everything they could to shut down my accounts and minimise the damage. We had the legal department chasing Australian representatives from Instagram, Facebook and Twitter. Harder than you'd think. It truly was the stuff of nightmares.

More and more friends were now texting me: 'Sam, I just looked at your Twitter, are you wasted?' and my personal favourite, 'Dude, what's happening? You've gone full Kanye?'

I wish I could've seen the funny side of it at the time, but I was really frightened. I thought about all of the personal messages and information they had access to. Not that there's anything too salacious in my inbox (mainly puns and cat pictures), but the scariest part was not knowing what might happen next. Perhaps this was only phase one of an even bigger takedown? Had I upset someone to provoke this? I'm not exactly a shock jock so I was confused as to who might have a beef with me. Other than opposition weathermen. Or actual meteorologists.

Mel, Vanessa and I were trying everything to regain control of my accounts. But it was hopeless. Without a contact from the platforms themselves, we had no control whatsoever. So I had to just sit there and endure the excruciating wait as more and more posts were uploaded from my accounts. After about ten tweets in Arabic, the hacker finally posted a tweet in English. It was a very simple two-word tweet that read, 'f**k you'. No context, no further information, just 'f**k you'. Ironically it's what I felt like saying to them.

The thing that made me even more furious was that the 'f**k you' tweet was actually getting a lot of likes. It received almost a hundred likes, more than most of my actual tweets. That was salt in the wound. My hackers' content had better social engagement and more cut-through than my own. Ouch.

In the end, it took us a week to regain control of my accounts. The first few days of that week were very difficult. The constant worrying was exhausting. I was also extremely anxious about what was going to happen next.

Towards the end of the week, I genuinely felt lighter. My head felt clearer. I think I was experiencing the benefits of not being so consumed by the constant noise of social media. I love social media; it's a platform where I can do and say whatever I want. I can talk directly to my audience with no interference. It's intimate and it's powerful. But I'm willing to put my hand up and say that sometimes I devote too much of my time and too much of myself to maintaining it, often at the expense of real-life interactions.

This hacking experience really made me question how much of my life I live via those accounts, and how reliant I am on both creating and consuming the content. Maybe this happened to teach me a lesson.

We spend so much time on our phones. On Instagram. And so much of that time is just mindless scrolling. I liken it to playing the pokies. We keep going back again and again because we have a few wins (i.e. we find a good piece of content) but a lot of it is pointless.

I remember being on a work trip at the Singapore Zoo. We didn't have a lot of time so we were driving through on a buggy tour. I almost missed a quick glimpse of an incredibly rare white tiger because my face was glued to my screen. I was on Instagram and watching an Insta story of some model I follow showing off her new earrings and telling people a codeword they could use for 15 per cent off. A FREAKING WHITE TIGER! Now, I'm sure the earrings are great, and I'm very happy for her, but that was a big reminder and a prime example of why I needed to find a better balance with my social media.

Above: This wasn't a photo shoot – just a standard Saturday for Coco and me. (Darren Leigh Roberts, Newspix)

Left: The picture I always send Loretta when she asks why I'm still single.

Below: Be very careful when googling this publication. (*Pussweek* magazine)

He's not posing. That's how The Human Emoji looks ALL THE TIME.

Right: Hate it when you go to the footy and get seated near the riffraff.

Below: We're just one big happy family at *Sunrise.* (Channel 7)

With Mum and Dad at Elton John. If only we knew a qualified weatherman who could have predicted that rain.

I'm patiently waiting for the inevitable offer from National Geographic for the rights to this shot I took at Uluru.

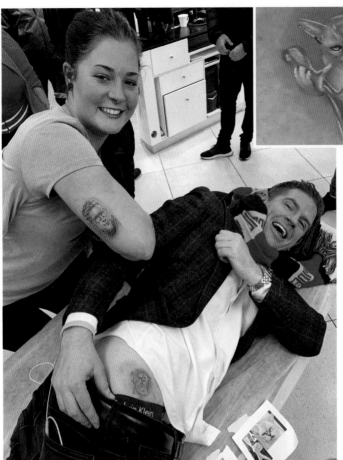

Above: It's true. I really do have a tattoo on my hip of my cat holding a Logie I didn't win.

Left: Danni smiling through the realisation that she's stuck with me for all eternity.

My elaborate technique of ensuring a good park in Rundle Mall.

Loretta using me as a decoy to avoid Delta's security. (Darren England, AAP Image)

Left: I was the only cast member asked to keep my clothes ON for *The Real Full Monty* promo shoot. (Channel 7)

Below: Seeing my 'Subtle Glow' tan for the very first time.

Showcasing the R U OK? wristband I wore for a year ... while incorporating a sneaky bicep flex.

To truly become a Wiggle, first you must be at one with the skivvy.

Half Man Half Cat, confusing children since 2019.

Above: Nikki Webster and me – the affordable Jay Z and Beyoncé.

Left: Playing it cool while waiting for Shania Twain to notice me.

Promo shot for my yet-to-be-funded Aussie romance, *50 Shades of G'day.*

You can learn a lot about a man from how he handles his hose.

Above: Where's Carol's right hand ...?

Right: Giving the ladies what they want: exposed, highly luminous ankles.

I don't think I've ever felt as relieved as I did on the day we regained complete control of all of my accounts. I sent flowers to Mel and Ness because I honestly didn't know how I could've handled the ordeal without them. They went above and beyond, and they both now have a handy fallback career as cyber security experts slash counsellors.

The hilarious part of this story is that the hackers managed to infiltrate every single one of my social media and email accounts, except one. The only account that was completely untouched was the one belonging to my cat, @lifeofmisscoco. Incredible. Even ISIS knew not to screw with Coco.

•

Two weeks after the hacking, I faced yet another ordeal, but this time it was self-inflicted.

Towards the end of every year, the *Sunrise* team are lucky enough to be invited to the residence of Kerry Stokes in Darling Point. It's even more picturesque than you can imagine. Beautiful leafy gardens, stunning harbour views and chirping birds that I presume have been handpicked as they tweet frequently enough to be cute but not so often to be annoying. Unlike my hackers.

Kerry – or Mr Stokes, as most of us call him – is the big, big boss, the chairman of the Seven Network. He and his wife, Christine, put on a spectacular afternoon of lunch and beverages. It truly is a privilege to be invited. I really should return the favour one day by inviting them over to my shoebox apartment in Darlinghurst where I can butcher their favourite songs in a #SamMacoustic guitar sesh and order them Nando's via Uber Eats.

It had been a very successful year, so the drinks and laughs were certainly flowing. Most importantly, it was a Friday. Anybody who works in breakfast TV knows that Friday is *the* day. Reaching Friday feels like you've climbed Everest and it's time to enjoy the view. The knowledge that there's no 4 a.m. alarm the next day brings a vibe that is equal parts joyous and dangerous. For me, on this occasion, it was dangerous.

We left the Stokes residence at around 5 p.m. and it's safe to say I was feeling rather jolly. I was certainly in no state to operate a forklift or any form of heavy machinery. A group of about eight of us decided to kick on for a few more drinks. Not the wisest decision I've ever made.

Fast forward a few hours and the good news was that I was home safely. However, there was a problem: I reached into my pocket to grab my phone and realised it wasn't there.

I checked the house; it wasn't there either.

I retraced my steps (not an easy thing to do after a long day on the wines), but even in my foggy disposition, I knew the grim reality. I'd lost my phone.

This was the last thing I needed after the hacking incident. I was so angry at myself. It was all my doing.

My housemate Ally was unbelievable. She reassured me that everything was going to be okay. She told me off for being too hard on myself.

'It's a simple mistake, Sam,' she said. 'You're human, these things happen. Everything is going to work out. It's just a phone.'

I knew she was right. But much like the hacking situation, which I was probably still coming to terms with, it made me realise how dependent I was on my phone. My whole life was in that little thing. All of my contacts, photos, personal messages. Everything.

Ally calmed me down to a level where I could at least go to bed. It was an awful night of broken sleep. The next morning I walked to the police station. I guess it was an act of desperation. I realised that, in the scheme of things, a lost phone was not an urgent priority, but they were very helpful.

We contacted the venue, the cab companies, and just generally put the feelers out. We even tried calling the phone a number of times but it was switched off.

Next I got on my laptop and sent Facebook messages to the workmates I'd been with the previous night. I asked if anyone had seen my phone. Unfortunately, none of them had. I was beginning to lose hope.

By this stage, I had hit a real low point. The combination of the hacking and now losing my phone in such quick succession had left me feeling more exposed than ever. Even more exposed than in *The Real Full Monty*.

Then, finally, some good news. My workmate Monica Lepore sent me a direct message saying that she'd called my phone and someone had answered. A man named Bryan had found my phone in a cab and had it in safe keeping. Monica told me his address and arranged for me to taxi over to his place and pick my phone up in an hour. I felt such a sense of gratitude. So, so lucky.

I arrived at Bryan's place in Cammeray and was greeted by a very friendly young man. My phone couldn't have landed in better hands. He told me it was on the floor of a taxi he got into the previous night. He'd taken it home and charged it. What a guy.

Bryan had noticed some notifications that mentioned my Instagram and he knew who I was, so he'd been trying to track me down. He'd sent me direct messages on Instagram but I didn't receive them because I only access Insta via my phone.

Basically, he'd tried everything in his power to return my phone to me.

I was trying my best to communicate how thankful I was, and how much it meant to me. Before I left I handed Bryan a hundred dollars cash. I said, 'I know it's not much, but it's something. I'd love for you to treat yourself to a nice dinner. It's just my little thank you for being a good human.'

Much to my surprise, Bryan refused to take the money.

'I did it because it was the right thing to do,' he said, 'and I'd hope that someone would do it if they found my phone.'

I appreciated where he was coming from, but I really wanted to give him that little thank you reward. By now it was becoming quite tense. It wasn't an argument, but it was definitely some sort of polite stand-off.

I had an idea. 'How about you take the money and donate it to the charity of your choice?'

All of a sudden, this story got very interesting. Bryan's response truly blew my mind. He said, 'Well, I actually run my own charity. It's an early intervention mental health not-for-profit called the Banksia Project.'

I remember this moment so clearly. I had goosebumps. I don't mean that figuratively, I literally had goosebumps and I could see them as I looked down at my arm.

I showed Bryan my yellow R U OK? wristband and told him I'd lost a friend to his battle with mental health. I told him I was an ambassador for R U OK? Day and that mental health was the cause I was most passionate about.

We both felt such an instant connection. We understood. He took the hundred dollars and promised me it would be going straight to the Banksia Project. Before I said goodbye, I told Bryan I'd love to host an event for his charity if they ever needed someone.

One week later I received a message from Bryan: 'Hey Sam, I completely understand that this is very short notice. But we're having a forum on mental health in the music industry on December 5 and I'd love you to host it.' I was delighted to be asked and told him it would be an honour.

The event was a big success. The conversation was open, honest and insightful. And that's what it's all about: creating an environment where people feel comfortable to speak up. To seek help when required.

I had a drink with Bryan and his team at the end of the night and we agreed to work together again in the future.

As I was heading home in the Uber, I realised the significance of the date. December the fifth. It was the eve of the anniversary of the day we lost Richard Marsland to his battle with mental health eleven years ago.

I eventually got home at midnight. December sixth. The day we lost Richard.

There was something beautiful about how it all lined up. I lost my phone. A random Good Samaritan found it. I offered him money. He wouldn't accept it. We eventually agreed to donate the money to his charity. He then asked me to host an event for his charity. The event fell almost to the day on the anniversary of when we lost Richard.

I know we look for meaning and symbolism with big life events, but I couldn't help but feel a sense of comfort. I felt that Richard had almost orchestrated this from above. I took it as a little nod from him to say that I was doing the right thing, and that my work on mental health was appreciated. That was a special feeling.

And, knowing Richard's sense of humour, if he did orchestrate it, I bet he found the bit where I lost my phone absolutely hilarious.

12

Logies

'Are you sitting down?'

It was a strange question to be asked by the executive producer of *Sunrise*, Michael Pell, in a rare late-afternoon phone call. It was Tuesday, 21 May 2019, and I was in a hotel room in Ipswich, Queensland, with The Human Emoji and my cameraman, Chris Lange. We were putting the finishing touches to an edit for a segment airing the next day. I assured Michael I was sitting down. He continued.

'I have some news, some very big news, Sam Mac – you've been nominated for the Gold Logie.'

I heard the words. I understood the words. But it took a moment for me to truly grasp the words. My reaction was eloquent and befitting of someone just nominated for the highest honour in Australian television.

'Holy shit!'

It was an extremely unexpected surprise. Michael went on to say some lovely things: 'This is a really big deal, Sam. *Sunrise* has never had a host nominated for gold in our twenty-year history. You're our first. It's great for the network, great for the show, and great for you. You deserve it, and we're all very proud of you. No matter what happens, this can't be taken away from you, you'll always be a Gold Logie nominee.'

I gave The Human Emoji an enormous hug. The nomination was recognition of his work just as much as it was of mine.

In true producer style he then sprang into action.

'I'm going to the bottle-o for some champagne,' he said. 'I'll be back in ten!'

The three of us then sat in a run-down Ipswich hotel room and shared a toast to the most exciting news of my career so far.

An hour or two later I went back to my room and had a quiet glass of champagne by myself. Hey, I don't have a drinking problem. It was a special occasion. And champagne doesn't keep well.

I wasn't allowed to tell a single person until Sunday, the day the nominees would be officially announced. But I desperately wanted to tell Mum and Dad. It was such a surreal feeling, sitting there, letting it all sink in. But having to keep it to myself. I was in disbelief.

I was even a little teary. Or perhaps that was just the champagne.

My whole career flashed before my eyes. Again, possibly the champagne.

But I started thinking about all of the people who'd helped me get there, all of the highlights, the lowlights, the places I'd visited.

Most of all, I thought about sacrifice.

Being nominated made me look at my life, my job and myself more analytically. It forced me to look back, something I don't do very often.

I thought about the hundreds of hours I had volunteered to create a community TV show while I was at uni. I thought about the risk I took, moving from Adelaide to Sydney for an eight-week contract. Even at the time, I knew I was making those decisions with a single focus: to follow my TV dream. If you don't try, you don't know.

I thought about 2011, when I quit my radio job in Perth to move back to Sydney. I didn't have another job lined up in Sydney, and my friends thought I was crazy, but I just knew I had to be there, yet again, to follow my TV dream.

I thought about all of the family gatherings, the weddings, the dates, the friends' birthdays, the midweek catch-ups that I'd missed out on, all because I was away, following my TV dream.

I thought about the 3.47 a.m. alarm that's woken me up more than a thousand times for *Sunrise*, all so I could follow my TV dream.

As I sipped the last bit of champagne, it occurred to me: I wasn't following my TV dream anymore. I was living it.

A few days after I received the news about the nomination, I was on the Gold Coast for the official nomination announcement. The organisers very kindly granted me permission to tell my family an hour or so before it became public.

It was a Sunday afternoon, so I knew Mum and Dad would be at my sister Paula's place. I called Paula and made sure she was in a private spot. I told her the news first. She was trying desperately to muffle her excited squeals.

Paula is one of my fiercest supporters and I love how much joy she gets from my career. I told her I was going to call Mum in ten minutes to tell her the news. Paula knew the drill: 'Oh cool, do you want me to film it?'

The video of this moment really makes me laugh. Picture Loretta, perched on the balcony, wind in her hair, and holding a glass of chardy containing such a generous pour there's probably around three standard drinks in it. 'I've only had one glass!' Classic Loretta.

Mum answers the phone and I prepare her for the news.

'Mum, I've got something really big to tell you – it's very exciting. I've been keeping it a secret, but I'm finally allowed to tell you.'

I'd barely finished my sentence and Loretta butts in, 'You're getting married!'

Wow. That would've been some secret, as I didn't even have a girlfriend at the time. Perhaps Loretta had been watching too much *MAFS*.

'No, I'm not getting married, Mum.'

Loretta loves a guessing game, so she immediately had a second bite at the cherry: 'I know, you're going to be a daddy!'

At this point I made a decision to never play guessing games with Loretta again.

'No, Mum, I'm not going to be a daddy. If you'll shut up for a second, I'll tell you my news – the news is, I've just been nominated for the Gold Logie.'

Loretta fired up. 'Oh my god, Sam, that's amazing. Congratulations!'

She sounded excited, she said lovely things, but I couldn't help but detect a hint of disappointment that I wasn't getting married or about to become a 'daddy'.

After that unexpected hit to my ego from my own mother, I rushed downstairs at The Star on the Gold Coast to the Logies announcement soirée. Richard Wilkins from the *Today* show and Sarah Harris from *Studio 10* hosted the event, and it was teeming with media and alcohol. A dangerously lethal combination.

I did a few red carpet interviews but was still forbidden from telling anybody else the news. Finally, after running through all of the categories, it was time to reveal the Gold Logie nominees. I had a few ideas who my fellow contenders would be, but I wasn't entirely sure. So when my name was read out next to the likes of Waleed Aly, Tom Gleeson and Amanda Keller, I was quite overwhelmed. I'm lucky enough to know those guys and they are well and truly the best in the biz. I know it's a cliché, but I was absolutely honoured to stand alongside them. As a battler from the suburbs of Adelaide, this was rather surreal.

After the function I headed back to my hotel room and called Mum and Dad for a proper debrief. We spoke for a good half an hour about my career and the nomination and how I was feeling. It was such a special conversation. I know Mum and Dad are proud of me, but to hear them say it repeatedly really filled my heart with joy.

There's an important lesson in that: don't just think people know how you feel because it's implied – say it. Sometimes people really need to hear the words. Or perhaps they don't need to hear it but they deserve to hear it. Say it.

By the time I got off the call with my parents the nominations had been made public, both on the news and on social media. My phone was going bananas. I had over a hundred text messages. Plus hundreds of tags and comments on Facebook, Twitter and Instagram. It was a bit of a spin-out. Messages from old school friends, workmates, even soccer pals who I hadn't spoken to since under-12s. Wonderful. It kind of felt like *This is Your Life*.

I also received beautiful congratulatory messages from friends and people in the industry I really admire, like Carrie Bickmore, Peter Helliar and my great mate Dr Chris Brown.

Just as I was sitting there feeling pretty good about myself, a direct message came through on Twitter that was the cherry on top of my nomination cake. Shaun Micallef! In my opinion, Shaun Micallef is the greatest comedic talent to ever come out of Australia. With the possible exception of Bob Katter (but his comedy is unintentional).

I grew up watching, studying, and marvelling at the inimitable humour of Shaun Micallef. I'd been lucky enough to meet and interview him a couple of times, and he always lived up to the pedestal I'd placed him on. To think that one of my comedy heroes would take the time to congratulate me was legitimately mind-blowing.

His message was very on brand for Shaun Micallef, hilarious and absurd. He wrote, 'Congratulations on the nomination, Sam. Well deserved. If you win, please do a long speech about Palestine.'

In the week leading up to the Logies, the team at *Sunrise* decided to send me on a political-style campaign, visiting five states in five days. The idea was that we'd do the show live from five of the biggest TV markets, with celebrity endorsements and a final push for votes.

At first I was a little unsure about it. I'm not against doing something self-indulgent if it's funny, but I was concerned this could be overkill. The *Sunrise* team, on and off air, were extremely passionate about it, though.

The Human Emoji and I decided that if we were going to dedicate a week of air time to this, it had to be ridiculous, it had to be completely over the top. The question we kept asking ourselves as we planned it was, 'Will it be entertaining for people who really don't give a shit about the Logies (i.e. most people)?'

The campaign launch on the Monday was in Sydney, at Milsons Point, with the Sydney Harbour Bridge providing a stunning backdrop. Former Gold Logie winner Ray Meagher, a.k.a. Alf Stewart from *Home and Away*, was there to give me an official endorsement.

'I've never asked for a vote for anything in me whole life,' he said, 'but I need you to vote for this kid, he's flamin' desperate.'

In the next segment I was joined by another member of Australian television royalty, Kamahl. He wished me luck for my campaign then rather cruelly started belting out 'The Impossible Dream'. The Human Emoji had requested a twenty-second snippet of the chorus, but that's not how Kamahl rolls. Roughly one minute into his performance I started to wrap the segment, but he just kept on singing. He even heckled me for attempting to end the cross.

'I'm Kamahl,' he said, 'you try and stop me.'

It was very loose, and exactly the sort of entertainment we'd hoped for.

(Side note: it was important I stayed in Kamahl's good books because I'd like to collaborate with him one day on a Christmas single, 'O, Kam-ahl Ye Faithful'. And therein lies the greatest pun in this entire book. Take a moment. You're welcs.)

There was one more surprise organised for day one of my campaign, and it was a biggie. You know it's serious when they put me in a blindfold. We love a big reveal. And The Human Emoji just happens to have a selection of blindfolds lying around the house. Coincidence?

Live on air, my blindfold was removed. I turned around to see fifty members of the Australian Girls Choir. They were singing 'Gold' by Spandau Ballet in perfect harmony. Behind them was an enormous Greyhound bus with a picture of Coco and me on it. Incredible scenes. I was well and truly blown away. On one side of the bus was the official hashtag, #MacItHappen, and on the other side in enormous gold letters it had my campaign slogan, 'Mac The Logies Great Again'.

It was hard to believe this was only day one of the campaign. We certainly launched with a bang.

After the show I raced across town for a few radio interviews including *The Kyle and Jackie O Show*, where I performed a take-down song about Tom Gleeson. Tom had been heckling the other nominees on his ABC show.

I think Tom's hilarious, and I was not surprised or offended by his attack videos at all, but the media were definitely trying to turn the narrative into something more sinister. Either way, it was already the most talked-about Logies campaign in years.

After the radio chat we headed to the airport and boarded the long flight to Perth. And before you ask, no, being a Gold Logie nominee does not automatically upgrade you to business. Not even premium economy. By the time I got to my hotel in Perth I was exhausted, and it was only Monday. The reality of five states in five days started to kick in.

The time difference meant my first cross the next morning was at 2.30 a.m. Perth time. We were live from 92.9, my old radio station in Subiaco. Understandably, this show was nowhere near as (M)action packed as the launch day, but it was quite heartwarming to have some of my old WA pals come and support me in the middle of the night (thanks Chris, Jeff, Lara, Adrian, etc).

The highlight of day two was sharing a montage that demonstrated my versatility as a presenter. We had a package cut together of the studio hosts introducing my segments. It doesn't sound overly entertaining, but when they're very tightly cut together you start to understand just how absurd this role is.

Here's a little taste of what was in the montage. For added effect, I recommend reading the following in the voice of Kochie or Sam Armytage:

'Sam Mac is at an avocado farm'

'Sam Mac is at a baby disco'

'Sam Mac is picking mandarins this morning'

'Sam Mac is at a retirement village'

'Sam Mac is at a birthing class in Dee Why'

'Sam Mac is learning Bollywood dancing'

'Sam Mac is riding a camel'

Hmm, I'm beginning to think I wasn't hired for my meteorological expertise ...

After the show I had five radio interviews and a photo shoot with my old mate Basil Zempilas. These days he's the Lord Mayor of Perth. But back when I lived in Perth and we hosted breakfast radio together, he was known by another illustrious title – he was a 'Perthonality'. Our photo appeared in the *West Australian* newspaper with the headline 'Up at 3 a.m. 132 flights a year. And no coffee'.

The fact that I don't drink coffee seems to blow people's minds. It's just never been part of my routine. I think because of my hours and the energy I exude on TV, people presume I must be knocking over a few early-morning lattes. So when I tell them I don't drink coffee, they react like I've just told them I eat babies. Their jaws drop. (I don't eat babies, by the way. The flesh is far too tender at that age.)

After a total of eighteen hours in Perth we headed to the airport in preparation for day three of our five states in five days tour. Wednesday morning was based at the Mabel Park State High School in Brisbane. A wonderful school with its own gym and hair salon – so you can get shredded and dreaded (a slogan they kindly declined when I offered it to them free of charge). But my favourite part of the school was its diversity. Their numbers are dominated by multicultural students. So many kids from such different backgrounds all working together.

The highlight of day three of my campaign was a segment with our former Minister for Foreign Affairs, Julie Bishop. Ms Bishop is one of the most formidable people I've ever met. She's super sharp, cheeky, and even ruthlessly scathing when necessary. It's important to remember here that all of the put-downs were tongue in cheek and we have the highest respect for one another. At least, I hope so.

The premise of the segment was to get Ms Bishop's expert analysis on how my campaign was travelling. I started by asking her for some honest feedback on my official slogan, 'Mac The Logies Great Again'.

She was not impressed. 'It's appalling,' she said. 'It'll never take off.'

I didn't have the heart to tell her it was already printed across the campaign bus and all official merchandise.

We were filming the segment at Kangaroo Point in Brisbane so Ms Bishop decided to put me through my paces with a stair run, push-ups and some boxing. During the stair run she physically pulled my arm to keep up the speed and told me I was 'pathetic'. While I was doing the push-ups she placed her foot on my back and attempted to physically push me into the ground. I knew she was savage, but this was another level. I should've shouted 'Pineapple!' (my safe word).

I decided to get my own back during the boxing. I asked her, 'Who do you picture while you're boxing? It's Dutton, isn't it?' That at least produced an awkward smile.

With the workout complete, Ms Bishop decided to talk strategy. 'You need to keep your eyes on the prize. In your case, it's a Gold Logie.' She then shrugged her shoulders and rolled her eyes at the camera.

I interrupted, 'Well, that was rather dismissive, your body language, it's almost like you undervalue the award?'

She continued, 'No, no, if that's your life goal, a Logie, then it is what it is.'

Next she decided to double down and get even more personal.

'Now, I've had a look at your social media. Too much cat. I know you love your pussy photos –' another knowing look to camera '– but people want to follow you, not pity you.' Wow.

The final piece of the segment was supposed to be an endorsement from one of the most powerful women in the country. This is legitimately what she said: 'He obviously needs all the support he can get. I know he's got loser written all over him, but please do it for the team.'

Julie Bishop had well and truly ripped me and my campaign to shreds. So with my tail between my legs (that's

an intentional cat pun, stop trying to change me, J-Bish), it was time to head to Melbourne for day four.

Federation Square was our base for the penultimate stop of our five states in five days. I was delighted to have so many loyal *Sunrise* viewers and fans come down to get involved in the Logies build-up.

A group of kids had hand-drawn an enormous poster of Coco and Catra. Very cute, although there was probably room on the poster for them to have included me as well. Just sayin'.

A long-time supporter named Cherie De Livera gave me a bottle of wine with my name on it. I bet I wasn't the first person to be holding a bottle of red in Fed Square at 6 a.m.

We even had a tap-dancing troupe from Glamour Puss Studios performing a special routine.

The Human Emoji and I pride ourselves on bringing colour and movement. A travelling circus. But we also place just as much importance on having heart. Making sure we're good humans and ensuring everyone feels included. It can be very nerve-racking for someone to get up early and come and meet us next to all of the cameras and lights. We want them to feel as comfortable as possible.

Over the past few years I'd built up an Instagram friendship with a young lad named Noah Callan. Noah is in a wheelchair and has cerebral palsy quadriplegia. But what

I admire most about Noah is his zest for life. I was thrilled that his mum could bring him in and we could finally meet in person.

Noah speaks via a system called eye gaze technology. It's absolutely brilliant. So, live on the air, I gave Noah a platform to say a few words, and this is what he said.

'My name is Noah Callan. I have cerebral palsy quadriplegia, but I don't let it affect me. I communicate with eye gaze technology, which means I can write and speak just by using my eyes. It's pretty cool, isn't it? Sam, every weekday, you wake up at 3 a.m.! How do you bloody do that? I don't see other nominees doing that. It's a credit to you, mate. You are a kind-hearted person who makes funny jokes to put smiles on people's faces every morning. Go to tvweeklogies.com.au to vote for this cat person weatherman, and mac the Logies great again.'

That meant so much to me. Not only to hear those beautiful words and have such a passionate supporter, but I was also extremely proud of Noah for delivering that under pressure, in front of a national audience. What a champion, and a great inspiration to others facing similar life challenges.

After radio interviews in Melbourne with Eddie McGuire, my great friend Wil Anderson and the always entertaining Brendan Fevola, it was off to the airport again. We arrived in Adelaide just after lunchtime, Thursday afternoon. It was no accident that we were wrapping up our campaign in my home town.

I raced straight from the airport to the 'Malls Balls' for a photo shoot. For those unfamiliar, 'Malls Balls' is the nickname for two stainless steel spherical sculptures in the middle of Rundle Mall. They're a couple of hundred metres from the Pig Statues. Yes, Adelaide is a gloriously weird place. Which was why no one really batted an eyelid when, early Friday morning, our enormous black Greyhound bus decorated with a picture of me holding my cat casually pulled into Rundle Mall. We'd made it to the final stop. Five states in five days.

But The Human Emoji had well and truly saved the best for last.

A few weeks prior I'd received a direct message from a young Adelaide woman named Danni Robson. 'I've decided to get a Sam Mac tattoo,' she wrote, 'and I just thought I should let you know.' I remember thinking it was kind of random, but also kind of awesome. So I wrote back to her and forwarded her message to The Human Emoji.

I'd actually met Danni earlier in the year during one of our segments, and I don't mean this in an offensive way, but she was totally normal! Generally if someone says they want to get a tattoo of you, you might wonder if they're a few sandwiches short of a picnic. But Danni was a beautiful, cool, funny, intelligent young lady. My initial response to her was, 'Really? Are you sure? Out of all the people in the world, you want to get a tattoo of me?'

The Human Emoji had arranged for her to get the tattoo for free, on the condition we could see it happen live on the air.

I interviewed Danni in the 6 a.m. cross in the tattoo parlour and asked her why she was going ahead with this. 'Well, I love waking up and watching you every morning,' she said, 'so in true Danni fashion I put it out to the universe, and then things escalated very quickly.'

I knew she'd decided to get my face tattooed on her arm, but I didn't know which photo it would be based on. Thankfully, she knew exactly what she wanted. 'There's one where you're wearing glasses and you look like a serial killer.' The team in the studio were in hysterics. Danni showed us the photo she was referring to. It was the *New Idea* photo shoot where I was wearing red spectacles and a burnt orange skivvy. And yes, this was the moment I learnt that my 'seductive face' was coming across as more of a 'serial killer face'. Noted.

As the segment was ending, Kochie threw in a late curve ball. 'Hang on, Sam Mac,' he said. 'Danni is getting a tattoo of you, and you've got a tattooist there – why don't you get a tattoo as well?'

He really put me on the spot. As I didn't have any tattoos at all, I gave a noncommittal response to buy some time: 'Let's focus on Danni for now, and we can discuss that further in the next cross in half an hour.'

The Human Emoji spoke to the tattooist, Mark Stewart. He assured us it was possible, and even sketched a few rough designs. I told them I was only willing to consider a tattoo of Coco. But it had to be small and somewhere on my body that was easily hidden. All of a sudden, half an hour had passed and we were back on the air watching Danni get my face tattooed on her arm. Danni was taking it all in her stride as she'd had a few tattoos in the past.

'You realise we're together forever now, Danni, we're bonded for life,' I said.

She seemed very relaxed about the whole thing. The tattoo was on the back of her arm and roughly the size of a tennis ball. But this is the best part: on the same arm she had two other tattoos, one of Prince and the other of Elton John. You can't make this up. So for the rest of her life, this woman will have to explain why on her arm she has two global icons of music and the *Sunrise* weatherman! I now refer to us as 'the big three'. And I take great pride in informing people that we have 'twelve Grammys between us'.

In researching this book, I touched base with Danni and asked her how the tattoo was going, a year or so on.

'People regularly grab my arm and say, "OMG you're the chick from *Sunrise*",' she said.

I asked if she had any regrets about tattooing my face next to Prince and Elton; she gave me a lovely response: 'You've earned your place. You have a naturally flamboyant and vivacious energy, so you fit right in. I have no regrets, not one. I think it's just a wonderful reminder of one of the most entertaining mornings of my life, and an overnight lifelong friendship.'

Now, back to the Friday morning before the Logies. Danni's tattoo was complete. What a surreal feeling looking at my own face permanently on someone else's body! The team were now wondering if I'd be getting inked myself. I decided to put it out to the viewers. We posted a photo on the *Sunrise* Facebook page of me standing next to tattooist Mark Stewart. He was holding the tattoo gun. I was holding a piece of paper that said, *If this photo gets 3000 likes in an hour, I'll get a tattoo of my cat.*

The photo received three thousand likes. In four minutes.

Still to this day, I'm unsure if that meant the viewers loved the relationship I have with Coco and wanted to see us connected forever or if they hated me and wanted to see me in pain. Possibly a little of column A, a little of column B.

I've never been a tattoo person. I've never fantasised or planned to get one. I just never considered myself a tattoo

kind of guy. I mean, I think they look great on other people. And I love the stories behind them, particularly the sentimental ones. But, at 7.30 a.m. on 28 June 2019, all of a sudden, I was a tattoo guy. With Loretta watching on, Mark Stewart masterfully inked my beloved cat Coco onto my right hip. Her face looks predictably unimpressed and she's cradling a Gold Logie. I must say, even though the decision was rushed, and for entertainment purposes, there was something so special about having Coco etched onto my skin for all eternity. I felt like I'd made the ultimate commitment to her.

As the exhausting and exhilarating campaign week was drawing to a close, there was one more piece in the jigsaw we needed to take care of. With a large crowd gathered in front of the campaign bus, I was joined by my mum and Paula. Kochie and Nat in the studio asked me if I was ready for Sunday night. I told them I was, but there was one more very important detail.

This is when I told Mum that she was going to be my plus one at the Logies and I gave her the gold envelope with her ticket in it. The crowd cheered and I gave Mum a big hug. She had absolutely no idea.

After the show it was quite chaotic. Loretta had become the break-out star of the morning. Radio stations wanted her, newspaper journalists wanted her, even random viewers were asking her for selfies. She took it all in her stride, with the assistance of her new bodyguard, Paula: 'Sorry, no more photos, Loretta has to go now, move back, thank you.'

Mum and I were interviewed for Adelaide's *Today Tonight*. It was my first time on *Today Tonight* and I breathed a sigh of relief as I realised I wasn't being featured in a story on dodgy fridge repairmen, online internet scams, or philandering love rats.

We also had an interview with my dear friend, the wildly talented Matt Gilbertson. He's the far less interesting half of his superstar alter ego Hans the German! Hans had appeared on the show earlier in the morning with another hilarious song. But by this time he'd done a Clark Kent-style transformation. Loretta was rather disappointed to encounter him out of character. Something I'm sure he's used to.

Matt asked Loretta what she would be wearing to the Logies on Sunday night.

'I only found out I was going an hour ago,' she said, 'so Paula's taking me shopping straight after this.'

Thankfully Loretta was in the epicentre of global fashion, Adelaide's Rundle Mall. Matt also asked Mum which celebrity she was most excited to meet. She paused for a moment, then said with great passion, 'Ooh, I really want to meet Edwina Bartholomew.'

At this point I butted in. 'Mum, of all the celebrities you could've said, you picked Eddy? She's on my show. She's my friend. I went to her wedding. I could arrange for you to meet her anytime! I could probably arrange for you to stay at her farm. Aim higher!'

Loretta was only warming up. Next she decided to bring up Tom Gleeson and the subsequent controversy surrounding him. By this stage there was a lot of media focus on his attack campaigns and some of the other nominees were not happy about his gung-ho (albeit comedic) approach.

Loretta wanted to chime in with her two bobs' worth: 'I'm not happy with him. He should not have done that. If he's reading this, Tom, I'm not happy with you at all.' As brazen as Tom Gleeson is, having Loretta on his case would've no doubt sent shivers down his spine. If he had one.

(I should reiterate, I'm a fan of Tom's and even had dinner with him in Byron Bay recently (#relatable). He's a very talented man who I respect greatly. The above was just a little bit of *Daily Mail* clickbait that I like to sprinkle throughout the book.)

After midday it was time for me to fly home to Sydney. All afternoon I received photo updates from Mum and Paula's shopping adventure in Rundle Mall. Mum was booked on a flight to the Gold Coast on Saturday morning, so the pressure was on to find her dress. Of course it was stressful for her and Paula to pick the right one with the clock ticking. But I could also feel how exciting it was for them. We all breathed a sigh of relief when they found 'the dress' at around 6 p.m. By this time they'd been in Rundle Mall for approximately twelve hours straight. Something you wouldn't even wish upon your worst enemy.

After such a hectic week, I spent the Saturday at home in Sydney relaxing and recharging. I went for lunch by myself and had a strum of the guitar. My job is all about people. I love it, but it can be very draining and that's why I really value that time to myself. I spoke to Mum every couple of hours to make sure she was okay. This was her first solo flight, her first time on the Gold Coast, and it would be her first time at a major awards night. That's exactly why I invited her. I wanted Mum to get a little taste of my life. I wanted to bring her into my work world. I also wanted to treat her to a special night as a way of saying thanks for everything she's done for me.

Mum was staying at the Sofitel, Broadbeach. That hotel was my home for three weeks during the Commonwealth Games in 2018. It's also my home away from home when I'm travelling to the Gold Coast for work. I stay there at least once a month. The staff are exemplary and they really do care. So when Mum told me they'd greeted her with a bunch of flowers and a card that read *Welcome Mrs Mac, we love having your son here, and now we're delighted to have you here too*, it really filled my heart with joy.

Mum called me again five minutes after the check-in to tell me that her room was 'stunning'. She went on to talk with passion for almost five minutes about the fruit platter they'd surprised her with: 'Oh Sam, it's so fresh. And it's so well presented. There's rockmelon, watermelon, pineapple, even some strawberries. And it's just so fresh. The staff here are amazing.' I didn't have the heart to tell her that all guests receive a fruit platter on arrival.

Sunday morning. Logies day. I woke up feeling more excitement than nerves. I just had one more important job to take care of before I hopped on my flight: I had to prepare Coco for hers. That's right, I arranged to take my cat to the Logies. Even as I write that, it sounds absurd. But we did it.

At 8 a.m. my legendary former housemate Jasmine Petty arrived at my place to take on the very important role of Coco's Gold Coast chaperone. I thought it was only fair that Jasmine received this honour given she created the @lifeofmisscoco Instagram account.

Jetpets literally rolled out the red carpet on the street as Coco was placed into their van. We enjoyed a brief, impromptu photo shoot (much to the confusion of my neighbours) then off she went. The next time I'd see her would be on the Gold Coast.

I got to the airport with plenty of time before my flight. That's a sentence I've never written before. I did a live cross into *Weekend Sunrise* with Basil and Eddy. They pointed out my obvious spray tan. I told them it was 'just the way the light was hitting me' but started to have flashbacks to *The Real Full Monty* Choc Mousse incident. But then I remembered I was heading to the Gold Coast. The spiritual home of fake tan. I'd fit in just fine.

It was quite a surreal feeling walking past the newsagency at the airport and seeing my face on the cover of *TV Week* magazine. I knew I didn't need to purchase one as Loretta would already have six copies in her extensive archiving system. Loretta keeps *every single article* ever written about me. If someone stumbled upon the archives in her spare room they'd think she was a serial killer tracking her next victim.

The Logies build-up had been a whirlwind. I hadn't really had time to stop and enjoy many of these moments. But as I checked social media and saw I had video messages of support from Tim Cahill (Australia's greatest ever footballer) and Eddie Betts (my all-time favourite Crow) I felt a wave of gratitude.

At 2 p.m. my little pre-Logies squad met in Jasmine's hotel room. Well, let's be honest, it was Coco's hotel room. The team at Sofitel Broadbeach granted special permission for the diva to stay in one of their deluxe suites. An absolute highlight of my Logies weekend was watching the waiter enter the room and deliver Coco her meal as she sat on the bed, her RBF (Resting Bitch Face) fully engaged.

The waiter, who was probably thinking, *I don't get paid enough for this shit*, then addressed her as if she was a human. 'Good evening, Miss Coco, thank you for dining with us at Sofitel, your dinner tonight is a carpaccio of scallops followed by local lamb loin, bon appétit.'

We were in hysterics as he then lifted the cloche, and after a few precautionary sniffs, Coco began devouring a meal that was probably better than what we were about to eat at the Logies.

My pre-Logies squad consisted of Mum, The Human Emoji, Jasmine and her boyfriend, Charlie, publicist extraordinaire Vanessa Till and, of course, Miss Coco. We toasted a glass of champagne to an unforgettable campaign and The Human Emoji ran through the plan for the next few hours.

Just when you thought my red carpet arrival couldn't possibly be any more elaborate, I decided the three of us should enter on a custom-built throne. I wanted Loretta and Coco to feel like queens, and queens sit on thrones. See, it's completely logical. I hadn't lost the plot at all.

Our friend Matt Hollywood (an illusionist we once almost killed in a live cross – story for another day, or book) kindly sourced a throne but now we were faced with the challenge of making it portable.

The Human Emoji hired three male models (who he just happened to have in his little black book) to carry the portable throne. They wore matching tuxedos and sunglasses. It was a vibe.

We decided to do a trial run at the hotel a few hours before the official red carpet commenced. It did not go smoothly. The uneven distribution of weight made the throne extremely heavy. The models could barely walk more than three steps without having to awkwardly set it down. It was not looking very regal. They can thank their lucky stars Catra wasn't invited.

But, after some trial and error, and a few close calls where we almost dropped Loretta onto the Sofitel car park, we were confident the dream could become a reality.

Ninety minutes later we met Kochie, Sam and the *Sunrise* crew for a drink in the Sofitel bar. The Channel Seven hair and make-up team had been kind enough to squeeze Mum into their busy schedule. So this was the first time I saw her done up and in her dress. She looked so beautiful. Now, I would've described her outfit as 'a green dress', but something told me that might not be enough detail for the Loretta fanbase out there. So, in writing this book, I texted her to ask who her dress was made by. This was her response:

> My dress was by Anthea Crawford. It was a long green gown with stunning beading on the shoulders. It was slim fitting with bell sleeves and a split on the left side. We found it at David Jones in the city. My shoes were from Nine West, they were black suede slingback shoes with an ankle strap. I had a black gathered clutch bag finished with a silver bar. I wore a classic black sparkly necklace with matching drop earrings. I felt like a princess wearing that gorgeous dress on a very special night with my son.

And that's precisely why Loretta is now considered a Style Icon among her fellow employees at Tip Top Dry Cleaners in Adelaide. You know what they say in the fashion world: London, Paris, Milan, Adelaide. But not necessarily in that order.

I wore a custom-made full velvet suit by the very talented Brent Wilson. And as I mentioned before, it was dirty green. And you can bet your life it was for Carol.

And so finally, after an enormous build-up, the moment had arrived. I didn't walk the Logies red carpet. That's so 2018. I *floated down* the Logies red carpet.

I remember making a point of taking a few seconds to look around and really appreciate the moment. There I was, squeezed into a portable throne with my darling mother by my side, and my precious rescue cat on my lap. We were gliding into the Logie Awards where I was nominated for Gold. It was quite the spectacle. Cameras were flashing, crowds were cheering, I felt on top of the world. Until about twelve seconds into our arrival the event organisers informed us we'd need to get off the throne for occupational health and safety reasons.

Oh yes, I should point out, we never thought to inform the organisers of our plan. Slight oversight. But it didn't matter. The indignity of being asked to get off our high horse (throne) actually made us all laugh hysterically. It made us truly appreciate how audacious our entrance was. Plus, by this time, we had the photos we wanted, and the male models were now roughly ten seconds away from passing out due to exhaustion anyway. As silly as it sounds, I'm super proud of that entrance. Mission (M)accomplished. We thought big, we took a risk, we made it fun and we did something memorable. That's what we're all about. We're in the entertainment business, it's our job to entertain.

After being unceremoniously dumped from our throne, it was time to walk the remainder of the red carpet like the other peasants. On a serious note, I was concerned Mum might be overwhelmed by all of the journalists and cameras and lights and shouting. This is part of my job, I'm used to this, but it was a very foreign environment for Mum. I started to get a little protective and was even holding her hand as I led the way down the carpet.

But I had nothing to worry about. Loretta handled it so effortlessly and took it all in her stride. She even started directing the photographers: 'We're just going to get a full body shot first, but we'll be with you in a moment,' she said. Like she was Patti Newton. Even in the interviews I was the one struggling to get a word in.

It brought me such joy to see her revelling in her new surrounds. There was a point where I suddenly worried that people might think she was my date. I made a point of addressing her as 'Mum' really loudly. I'm sure a few people must've glanced over and thought, *Geez, who's the cougar with Sam Mac?*

And if I thought Loretta dominated the red carpet, that was merely a warm-up for when she was let loose on the Logies itself. We entered a room full of the most powerful and well-known people in Australian showbiz and here was Loretta from Tip Top Dry Cleaners in Adelaide absolutely owning it. We had a photo with myself, Mum and Grant Denyer and Loretta said, 'I finally got a picture with my favourite weatherman.' Ouch, Loretta.

Next, she spotted Delta Goodrem. 'Oh look, there's Delta, I'd better go and say a quick hello,' she said. Like she was just catching up with an old friend. I think Mum was becoming a victim of that age-old scenario where you think because you love and feel a connection to a celebrity that they'll reciprocate your excitement. I've been there. Shania Twain.

The champagnes were flowing and Loretta was on a rampage. The hashtag #LorettaAtTheLogies was getting some real traction. There was a detective who won a Logie for an ABC show. Mum was obviously a fan because I saw her chewing his ear off after he'd won. I was sitting on a table with Channel Seven execs so I had a quiet word with Mum to also show some passion for Seven shows. 'You love *Home and Away*, don't you, Mum?' I said. I don't think she even heard me. She was still staring at Delta.

Her celebrity-spotting adventure wasn't over yet. Loretta then made a beeline for Tracy Grimshaw: 'Hello, Tracy, I'm Sam's mum.' I don't think poor Tracy even knew which Sam she was referring to. But she happily smiled for a selfie.

One of the best moments, though, was when Loretta decided to head to the other side of the room because she needed to tell Kerry O'Brien 'he's doing a good job'. Just five minutes prior he had been inducted into the Logie Hall of Fame. I think he knew he was doing a good job. And he probably wanted to celebrate with his close friends and family. But Loretta was on a mission, and she was unstoppable.

In true Mum style, Loretta still managed to make her brief conversation with Kerry O'Brien about her son: 'Sam's done so well. We always knew he'd do something on TV. He used to make little videos as a kid. We're all very proud of him.'

Thankfully Kerry O'Brien was such a gentleman, and I politely wound up the conversation for him.

'Come on, Mum, I think Delta's free,' I said.

Sitting on our table at the Logies were Kochie, Sam, Nat, Eddy, Beretts, Michael Pell, Vanessa Till and Craig McPherson. It was the first time in five years the entire on-air team had attended together, and it meant a lot to have them there supporting me. The nomination was also recognition of the team we've built and the moments we've created together. Michael is fiercely loyal to his team, and I'm extremely grateful for the content risks he's allowed me to take, even in my early days on the show. He believed in what we were doing. And, as mentioned earlier, it was Craig (along with Stefan Mitchell) who brought me over to Seven from Ten. So it was fitting that he was there too.

On my right was The Human Emoji and on my left was my mum. Perfect. By this time, Coco was back in her luxury hotel suite so she wouldn't be bothered by fans.

Pete Helliar had a friendly dig at me as part of the official broadcast: 'A weatherman is up for the Gold Logie.

It's Sam Mac. He has to be on drugs. How can he be so happy, getting up at an ungodly hour to go to a preschool in Canberra and do Bollywood dancing with a bunch of kids with ADD?' I should point out Pete was dressed as a Gold Logie as he made that joke. And as funny as it was, it was actually a rather accurate snapshot of my role. Pete and I have been mates for years, so I was certainly not offended.

I could see the camera hovering near our table to get cutaway shots of me during that bit. I decided it would be funnier if I was stony faced and gave him absolutely nothing. I just sat there with a bored, unimpressed look on my face. Kind of like Coco's. On the third cutaway I even took a big bite of the huge chocolate brownie that had just been served for dessert. It got a big laugh in the room and was quite delicious. Win-win.

Then, finally, it was announcement time. So many people were asking me through the night if I was nervous. I very rarely get nervous – if I do it's more likely to be a touch of anxiety about things going well – but I'm confident in my ability, and I'm open and ready for things to go wrong. As they often do in my segments. The fact I had Mum there gave me a different focus for the night. I just wanted to make sure she had a great time, so it kind of took my mind off why we were there. I felt very relaxed.

The delightful Rebecca Gibney was doing the honours. 'The winner of the Gold Logie is ... Tom Gleeson!'

I remember feeling a slight twang of disappointment in my gut. But it was very fleeting. Just a second or two, then I felt relief that we had an outcome and genuine happiness for Tom. His speech was loose, and very funny: 'This represents a joke to me. But I'm a comedian. I like jokes. People need to lighten the f**k up,' he said.

I know that some people felt his campaign and subsequent speech were undermining the awards, but I respectfully disagree. Tom is a comedian. He makes jokes. I think the wonderful thing about this Logies campaign, and part of why people took notice, was that the nominees were so diverse. And they approached the campaign in their own style, showcasing their own unique personalities. How boring would it be if everybody handled it the same way, and simply said it was an honour to be nominated? Snoozefest.

If I'm being completely honest, I wanted Amanda Keller to win. I admire her warmth and humour. She's got heart, and she's razor sharp. She's real, and I think she's such a well-rounded person and performer. She's also a personal friend of mine so I'm slightly biased.

I was blown away by the hundreds and hundreds of messages I received on social media after the announcement.

Really beautiful compliments from strangers on why they'd voted for me, and congratulations for being a nominee.

Some people seemed genuinely devastated: 'We voted for you so many times, I even let my kids stay up to see who won, they were crying,' one mother wrote. Others were checking on my welfare. 'Sam, I can't believe you didn't win, are you okay?' one lady asked. And one shop owner in South Australia had gone above and beyond: 'Sam, you deserved to win. We all voted for you. We handed out pamphlets of you in our shop.' I felt that wave of love from my supporters, and I'll always be thankful for that.

It was the highest-rating Logies in many years. I think the controversy surrounding the Gold ultimately made people care about the Logies again. It was divisive. It became like a sporting contest. Which team are you on? But most importantly, it was entertaining. And that's what it's supposed to be. So that's why it was a success.

With the formalities out of the way, I could now unwind and have a few drinks.

'You deserved to win, Sam,' said Mum, adhering to her Parenting 101 handbook. I loved having her by my side and introducing her to my world and many of the people I consider dear friends. By this stage, people were coming over because they wanted to meet her!

My mate, and Logie winner, comedian Dilruk Jayasinha gave her a big hug and told her she looked stunning. Then old mate Pete Helliar came over: 'I'm just here to get a selfie with Loretta if that's cool?' It made Mum's night. It made *my* night.

Loretta really did come in like a wrecking ball. Even on the minibus ride home she was still inflicting damage. 'And what do you do at Channel Seven?' she asked the lady sitting next to us. Now ordinarily that question would be absolutely fine. But not so much when you're asking that question of Emily Symons a.k.a. an acting legend who has played Marilyn on *Home and Away* for roughly 30 YEARS! Ahh, Loretta. Time to have a lie-down.

On Monday, 1 July, when I got home, I needed an afternoon nap. I was exhausted. I was woken up by my door opening and Jasmine calling my name. She was there to return Coco. So, still half asleep, I made my way down the stairs.

'How are you?' I said.

Her response was rather hesitant. 'Okay,' was all she said. Something wasn't right.

'Just okay?' I asked.

'Well, there's been a bit of a mix-up,' she replied.

I was very fragile, and a little bit disorientated having just woken up. All I knew was that she was supposed to be here to return Coco. My heart skipped a beat.

I got to the lounge room and I saw she was holding a white fluffball that had curly hair. Its face was turned in the opposite direction. It was roughly the same colour and size as Coco, but it wasn't Coco.

'Where's Coco?' I asked.

Jasmine nervously responded, 'She's in Adelaide, but they sent this one instead. There's been a mix-up. I'm sorry.'

The wrong pet was actually a dog.

'What the hell?' I said. I was so confused. And, remember, extremely fragile.

Then the driver from Jetpets chimed in. 'Yeah, this never happens, mate, it was just a miscommunication.'

By this point I'm very awake. I stared Jasmine down.

'Are you joking?' I said.

Then she burst out laughing. She couldn't keep up the lie.

I was now completely hunched over, in disbelief. 'I'm going to kill you. And the dog.'

In true Jasmine style, she thought she'd play a little prank on me while I was vulnerable. The dog belonged to the guy from Jetpets and they just did the ol' switcheroo. Of course, they filmed the whole thing. We then went outside and retrieved Coco from her cage in the Jetpets van. And all was well in the world again.

In the following days, after the Logies, I finally had time to read and respond to the unbelievably kind messages of support I'd received. There were hundreds on Instagram, Facebook and my text messages. It was quite overwhelming.

Most people seemed to feel an obligation to tell me I meant something to them, like I would be low on confidence after not winning. I appreciated the sentiment, but I was feeling great. There were a few gems that stood out. Like the lady who told me her mum had passed away two weeks ago. She said, 'Seeing you walk the red carpet with your mum was the first time I'd smiled since Mum passed. Thank you for treating your mum the way mums should be treated.' That one really moved me.

Another special message was from a former Victorian police officer. A guy named Keith who suffers from PTSD. He wrote the following: 'You may not have won the award, but to me you'll always be a winner. Your segments and energy have been a huge part of me having a positive start to my day for the first time in a long time. You've become part of my routine. You've helped me reach a point where I can now hold down a job again.' Magic.

But, ultimately, the Logies experience for me will always be about Loretta. It was one of the best decisions of my life to take her as my plus one. I was so proud to have the most important woman in my life gliding and then walking down that red carpet with me. And, as the dust had settled on the Logies chapter, after I'd replied to all of the beautiful messages of support, I received the knockout blow from my dear mum ...

I had such an amazing time, Sam. And I forgot to tell you, I wore your Nana's opal ring. So she was there with us also. xx

That well and truly hit me for six. Mum's parents, my grandparents, are no longer with us. And to know that Mum wore my nana's ring, a ring that my grandad made for her, was more important than winning any trophy. So special.

All in all, an incredible and emotional ride. The Logies truly did feel like my wedding night. Except the bride left me at the altar for Tom Gleeson.

13

Wiggles

I'm backstage at Sydney's International Convention Centre. The high-pitched screams of five thousand kids are echoing around the stadium. I'm nervous. What's wrong with me? I hardly ever get nervous.

But the magnitude (Macnitude) of what I'm about to do has finally kicked in. It's 2019 and I'm about to perform my own song onstage with the most successful children's entertainers of all time. I am about to become a Wiggle!

I run through the song a few more times in my head. I'm avoiding eye contact with the backstage staff as I don't want them to know how nervous I am.

There's a tiny monitor next to the curtains; on it I can see Emma the Yellow Wiggle performing her ballet song, which means I'm on stage next.

I close my eyes for a few seconds to visualise what I'm about to do.

'Wake up, Jeff!' shouts one of the tech assistants into my ear. Classic Wiggles humour. Or he genuinely thinks my name is Jeff.

A few more deep breaths and I allow myself a brief smirk in appreciation of the absurdity of my life. Have I mentioned I'm nervous? Seriously! Nailing this moment really matters to me. There's only one thing worse than disappointing a child, and that's disappointing five thousand of them *and* The Wiggles simultaneously. I don't want to be that guy.

I haven't felt this nervous since *The Real Full Monty*. But don't worry, kids, today I'll be keeping my pants ON.

My path to Wiggledom actually started several years earlier, in my second year on *Sunrise*. And it was an Australian icon who set me on it.

One morning we were planning to do our crosses live on the Sydney Harbour Bridge. The day before the climb, I had an idea. I said to The Human Emoji, 'The Sydney Harbour Bridge is an icon, Nikki Webster is an icon, two icons are better than one icon, so let's invite Nikki Webster onto the bridge to sing her 2001 hit "Strawberry Kisses"!' These are the types of phone calls my producer has to deal with on a daily basis. No wonder he has no hair.

The world fell in love with Nikki Webster via the Sydney 2000 Olympic Games opening ceremony. That little girl in the bright pink dress stole the show as she glided through the night sky in front of 2.1 billion people globally. We wouldn't see ratings figures like that again until I appeared on the Channel Ten breakfast show *Wake Up*. (Approximately seventy-five people will get that reference, which sadly was also about the number of viewers who watched the show.)

This was definitely a long shot. Why would Nikki Webster agree to perform with a weatherman on top of the Sydney Harbour Bridge? Thankfully Sean is just as twisted and persuasive as I am. We're constantly pushing each other to bring something unique to the show.

Sean responded enthusiastically, 'I love that. I have no idea what she's up to these days but I'll give it a go. Where do you think I can find her?'

'I read somewhere that she runs her own dance school,' I replied.

Sean made the call.

'Nikki Webster School of Dance,' said the voice on the other end of the phone. 'Nikki speaking.' Bullseye! It turned out that finding Nikki Webster was much easier than finding viewers for a Channel Ten breakfast show circa 2013.

Sean introduced himself and said, 'This is a bit of a strange request, but Sam Mac absolutely loves you and is keen to have you on the show. We're wondering if you'd like to perform with us tomorrow morning … on top of the Sydney Harbour Bridge?'

'That's such a ridiculous idea,' said Nikki, 'but why not?'

I was extremely excited when Sean told me Nikki was in. It reminded me of primary school when you'd get your mate to ask a girl out for you rather than doing it yourself. And then if she said no, you'd pretend to know nothing about it and claim that you never wanted to ask her out in the first place. Or was that just me? Writing a book is cheap therapy for such questions.

Okay, back to Nikki Webster. I didn't want the other hosts to know our plan. I was adamant it needed to be a surprise that unfolded live on air. There's nothing better than genuine surprise and authentic reactions. Our team are TV hosts, not professional actors.

I honed this technique over many years in radio. I even have a motto to go with it: 'If it didn't happen on air, then it didn't happen.' The sentiment behind it being that there's no use in someone having a big entertaining reaction unless that reaction happens on air and everybody gets to enjoy it. Yet again it comes back to authenticity.

That's why I often ask Sean not to tell me all of the details about activities or guests he has planned for our segments. It regularly provides the best on-air moments. The audience is smarter than people give them credit for and I believe they can tell if a moment is too contrived. Of course, that involves a lot of trust between Sean and me. But I'm completely fine with Sean keeping a secret from me if it means the audience gets the best end product. Unless, of course, that secret is bungee jumping. #Never4get

So, within sixteen hours of concocting that wild idea, I was on top of the Sydney Harbour Bridge standing next to Australia's sweetheart Nikki Webster.

I think it's important here that I talk about risk-taking. As I mentioned above, it was only my second year on *Sunrise*, and at this stage I was still finding my groove. Unleashing something as extravagant as this live on air could very easily go horribly wrong. But with great risk comes great reward.

'Ladies and gentleman, this morning I'm giving you two Australian icons for the price of one. Welcome back the one and only ... Nikki Webster!'

I gestured to my left. The camera panned to reveal Nikki Webster. It was a beautiful Sydney morning. The sun was glistening behind her and we could see the Opera House in the distance. *Three* icons for the price of one!

Judging by the clapping and cheering in my earpiece, it was a pleasant surprise.

'Wowwww! Hang on – why is Nikki Webster on the Harbour Bridge?' asked Sam Armytage, in an excited yet mildly confused tone. Perfect.

Before there was time for any further questions, Nikki launched into singing 'Strawberry Kisses' – not the original version, though. It was an updated version featuring my very own rap sequence: 'My girl Nikki Webster, where have you been? Since you flew into our hearts when you were just thirteen. That day in September, Australia remembers, it was the year 2000 but it's with us forever. Now she's back onstage, with an emcee on a minimum wage, but ignore the haters, the trolls, the disses, and always believe in Strawberry Kisses.'

The video was posted on the *Sunrise* Facebook page and ticked over a million views within twenty-four hours. Thousands of shares. The comments were joyous: 'OMG, I was obsessed with Nikki Webster when I was 12'; 'This is the greatest piece of television I've ever seen'; 'I'd forgotten how much I needed Nikki Webster in my life.'

Even the media were jumping on our moment, with news.com.au calling it 'the comeback of the millennium' and Scoopla describing it as 'lit'. This was obviously during the eight-week period where saying 'lit' was considered socially acceptable.

Unfortunately not all of the feedback was positive, with the news.com.au piece suddenly turning on me and describing my rap as 'an act of unnecessary aggression against our ears'. Ouch. It got worse, with Pedestrian reporting, 'Webster was at the top of the Harbour Bridge and, for some reason, accompanied by rapping Dad/Weatherman Sam Mac.' Dad? Wow. The rap game is tough, man. So many haters. Now I know how 2Pac and Biggie felt.

After such an enormous response, we decided to take things even further.

A week later Nikki and I were in the Triple M recording studio to 'lay it down'. Because, obviously, when you think Triple M, you think Barnesy, AC/DC and Nikki Webster. The big three. Tradies go mad for those strawberry kisses, bro. We all know that.

Truth be told, we recorded at Triple M because my mate Mike 'Sideshow' Andersen agreed to produce the song in exchange for a carton of beer. That's much more on brand for Triple M. And a sneaky insight into modern TV budgets.

Next, we shot the entire video clip in a day. First up, dancers on the sand at Bondi Beach. Then my personal favourite, back at Stadium Australia, the scene of the 2000 Olympics opening ceremony. It's where Nikki's life changed forever.

This time the stadium was completely empty except for Nikki's beautiful daughter, Skylah, who we included in the clip dancing with her mum in the middle of the stadium. Adorable.

The video clip went live and, yet again, we cracked a million views. The song even made it into the iTunes top 10, peaking at number 8.

We agreed to donate all proceeds from the song to the Starlight Children's Foundation. Starlight do an incredible job bringing joy to seriously ill and immunocompromised children. I've been lucky enough to work with them many times over the years and it's such a precious thing to see a child forget about what they're going through, even for a day. I love seeing the faces of the mums and dads and brothers and sisters on these days too. It means the world and it's quite magical.

So it was a very proud moment when Nikki and I handed Starlight a novelty-sized cheque for ten thousand dollars. Also, getting around with that kind of cash made me finally feel like the rapper I'd always dreamt of becoming.

It was an unforgettable launch to what will clearly be a long career for me in the rap game. I'm living proof that you can be both gangsta and charitable. Ya feel?

That experience marked the first example of me doing something truly out of the box – we pushed the limits of what you'd expect to see in a weather segment. Because it worked, and resonated with the audience immediately, I felt the producers at Seven started to really trust me. It was a pivotal moment because it gave me licence to take more risks.

I was ecstatic. I knew it had opened the door for us to make more memorable TV in the future. And I desperately wanted our segments to be noticed.

I have this theory that, particularly with breakfast TV, most viewers are only half watching. They're ironing their shirt, brushing their teeth, making breakfast for their kids. My modus operandi for this role was to get noticed. To put breakfast TV in the foreground. To have something on screen that was so absurd or intriguing that the viewers simply had to stop what they were doing and give you their undivided attention.

That morning with Nikki Webster gave me the confidence to back my instincts and take those big risks. The adrenaline rush that accompanies a big risk that pays off is hard to describe. I can live off that for weeks. It's a magical feeling and I think ultimately it's what drives me to keep doing what I do. In search of the next moment. The next buzz.

Skip forward a few years to 2019 and after the high of being nominated for the Gold Logie I decided to take a week off. I felt an enormous sense of achievement, but also slightly lost. Had I done all I could do with the weatherman role? Was that nomination the perfect full stop to my time on the show? Should I start to focus on what might be next?

These were the questions racing through my mind as I enjoyed some downtime on Hamilton Island. The Logies experience was an absolute whirlwind. From the unexpected nomination to the national tour, the countless interviews, the nonstop planning and preparation, and the night itself. A surprisingly emotional month. I thoroughly enjoyed it, but it was extremely high pressure and ultimately physically and psychologically draining. I had nothing left in the tank. It was one of the biggest experiences of my life, but little did I know, things were about to get even bigger. And Wigglier.

I remember exactly where I was when I received the Instagram notification. I was at my favourite brekkie spot in Sydney's Darlinghurst, the Stop Valve cafe, when the words 'new direct message from Anthony Blue Wiggle' appeared on my screen. Oh my.

I was secretly hoping that fellow diners would catch a glimpse of my screen, thereby giving me an opportunity to confirm at an unnecessarily loud volume that, yes, I was tight with The Wiggles. Whatevs, no biggie.

My excitement level was akin to when an attractive lady slides into my DMs. I know what you're thinking: *Have you ever had an attractive lady slide into your DMs, Sam?* The answer is yes, thank you very much, yes, I have. And I generally respond to them by politely declining their requests for Dr Chris Brown's phone number/address.

So I'm staring at my phone, letting the moment sink in. Anthony the Blue Wiggle has slid into my DMs.

I open the message and after a few lovely compliments, he wrote the following sentence, which I'll remember for the rest of my life: 'We'd love to have you in at Hot Potato Studios for a jam sometime!'

First of all, yes, their studio is legitimately called Hot Potato Studios. Second ... wowsers!

I immediately screenshotted the message just in case Anthony had second thoughts and reneged on the offer.

I also needed that visual evidence for when I eventually told this story to ANYONE IN THE ENTIRE WORLD WHO WOULD LISTEN.

I didn't want to appear too keen by replying straightaway, so I decided to leave him on 'seen'. For approximately forty-five seconds. Then I caved.

I told him I'd love to visit and that my producer would lock it in soon.

Sean and I are constantly throwing around potential story arcs for the show. The idea of me releasing a children's single was one we'd been sitting on for more than a year. This had to be the moment. Within a week of that Instagram chat, it was confirmed that we'd be doing the show live from Wiggles HQ to promote their upcoming Australian tour.

I distinctly remember being quite hungover the day before this was all supposed to play out. You might say I was 'under the weather'. But I knew this might be my only opportunity to share my songwriting skills with The Wiggles. So I spent six hours of that hungover Sunday trawling YouTube for royalty-free music and eventually writing not one but two children's songs.

The first one was a jaunty autobiographical ditty creatively titled 'Sam the Weatherman'. The second tune was a slightly more abstract piece about a young boy who slowly discovers that he's not a regular boy at all – he is, in fact, morphing into a 'Half Man, Half Cat'.

The morning arrived. These are the days I live for. These are the days I beat the alarm clock. I feel a different energy on days like this. It reminds me of how I used to feel as a kid on Christmas morning. I didn't want to sleep any longer. I just wanted the sun to rise so I could attack the day and open my presents. In this case, The Wiggles were my presents. Let's just brush over the fact I'm approximately thirty-five years past the age of their target demographic.

Hot Potato Studios are located in a suburb called Bella Vista, approximately thirty kilometres north-west of Sydney CBD. Next door you'll find a yoga studio, a McDonald's and a Woolies. Ahh, the glitz and glamour of showbiz!

Hot Potato Studios really are the Abbey Road of children's entertainment. As I walked through the hallway I was reminded of just how big these guys are. The walls are decorated with gold records, decades' worth of concert posters, and framed photos of The Wiggles with everyone from Chuck Norris to Shaquille O'Neal. Now *that* is broad appeal.

The first chat piece we did on air with the entire band was a lot of fun. We were in the props department and I discovered a hip flask near Anthony's blue skivvy. Salacious!

'I've always wondered how you have so much energy on stage,' I said.

After a few more laughs, Anthony asked if I'd like to join in on the next performance wearing a bird costume. Obviously, when a Wiggle asks you to wear a bird costume, the correct response is, 'Please hand me my feathers.'

After the elaborate blue feathers were attached and I'd miraculously squeezed into my tights, it was time for me to play 'rare exotic bird'. That's another sentence I never thought would appear in my first book.

I danced enthusiastically next to The Wiggles, flapping my wings with gusto for all of Australia to see.

'Maybe you can be Mr Wolf in our next cross,' Anthony suggested. I must point out that when Anthony 'asks' something at Wiggles HQ, there's not much of a question about it. He's the OG (original gangster) Wiggle and he knows the score. He also brings a childlike enthusiasm that you just want to be a part of.

Ten minutes later, thanks to their amazing wardrobe department, I'd made the transition from rare exotic bird to Mr Wolf. Yeah, I've got range, whatevs.

One of the most important traits you can have as a performer or host is a willingness to take ideas and run with them.

I studied two levels of improvisation at a wonderful school called ITS (Improv Theatre Sydney). The key philosophy of improv can be whittled down to just two words: 'yes, and ...' That means, when someone presents you with an idea or a comment or a story, not only do you accept it (yes), but you then add to it (and). Most of the best performers and entertainers instinctively do this. It's a generosity of spirit. It's keeping the ball in the air. The alternative is to block ideas or shut people down. I wouldn't recommend that approach unless you're looking for a gig on Sky News. Zinger.

I mentioned improv above because it's an enormous part of what I do. And on this particular morning, 'yes, and' was exactly how I was responding to whatever The Wiggles were throwing at me. I knew, in the back of my mind, that by embracing their ideas, it was going to put me in the best position for them to eventually embrace mine.

It was time for me to take my calculated risk. I casually told The Wiggles that I'd jotted down a few kids' songs of my own and I'd love to get some honest feedback in the next cross. They were instantly on board. Yes, and.

Minutes later I was in the booth performing thirty-second snippets of the two children's songs I'd written only twenty-four hours earlier (while hungover). Watching on from the control room were The Wiggles, global icons of children's entertainment. Watching on from their lounge rooms were hundreds of thousands of Australians via *Sunrise*. Pressure makes diamonds.

'Sam the Weatherman' received a warm response and a few polite laughs, but it was 'Half Man, Half Cat' that stole the show.

'That song is a hit,' said Anthony as he flashed his trademark smile. He went on: 'Kids all over the world know cats and they understand them. The song tells a great story and it's a unique concept, particularly once you add the costumes and fun.'

Then things escalated. Live on air, Anthony had a proposition: 'We'd like to invite you to perform "Half Man,

Half Cat" at one of our stadium shows later this year,' he said.

I was genuinely shocked. This was my Susan Boyle moment. I couldn't contain my excitement.

'I'm joining The Wiggles!' I shouted.

By this point we'd finished our live commitments with *Sunrise* and had started packing up. Anthony had other ideas.

'Hey, guys, if you have an hour or so, we could record vocals for the song and even shoot a video clip if you want?'

Unbelievable.

The next hour was a blur and an experience I still have to watch video of to confirm it actually happened. Purple Wiggle Lachie coached me on the song in the studio. Red Wiggle Simon then loaned his smooth baritone backing vocals to the track I'd written. Yellow Wiggle Emma faced the biggest challenge of her career, teaching me some form of acceptable dance choreography. And Blue Wiggle Anthony rallied us all together in their custom-built TV studio to shoot the video clip. We only did three takes. Wide shot, mid shot and roaming. I hadn't even memorised the lyrics yet, to the song I'd written! So I had them behind the camera on cue cards during filming.

It gave me a spectacular crash course in how The Wiggles machine works. Truly astonishing.

As we were on our way out the door Anthony still wasn't finished.

'Mate, we want to distribute this properly so I'd really like to sign you with Wiggly Tunes,' he said. 'I'll send the contract over to you today.'

'Yeah, of course, Anto,' I responded, pretending I knew what Wiggly Tunes was and also pretending I was now familiar enough to refer to him as Anto.

It turned out Wiggly Tunes was The Wiggles' record label. Just like that, I was a signed artist!

I distinctly remember standing in the car park of Hot Potato Studios with The Human Emoji just looking at each other in pure disbelief. It takes a lot to shut us up, but we were both absolutely dumbfounded. It felt like a dream. Not only had we wrapped one of our favourite mornings of live crosses, but we'd also recorded a complete song and video clip with The Wiggles, and it wasn't even 10 a.m.

Although the morning played out like a dream, there was never any guarantee that I'd get that opportunity to share my songs with The Wiggles. We never know how mornings like that are going to go – there are publicists involved, timelines, breaking news, things get dropped. There are so many variables.

But, much like with Nikki Webster, I'd prepared something just in case, and when I saw the opening, I went for it with all guns blazing. I took the risk.

There's a saying that luck is what happens when preparation meets opportunity. Some people might say that I had that goal and 'manifested' it. I think it's a bit of both. If I hadn't taken the time on that hungover Sunday to write the songs, I wouldn't have had anything up my sleeve to show The Wiggles. And when that opportunity presented itself, I wouldn't have had anything ready that would inspire them enough to invite me to record the song, the video and join them on tour. The Wiggles are big-time – they don't need a pesky weatherman hanging around trying to join in. But, with the songs I'd prepared, they could see my passion, they could see I'd taken a risk, and there was enough of a spark there for them to reward it.

'Half Man, Half Cat' was uploaded to The Wiggles' official YouTube channel and received half a million views within a week (presumably from kids who accidentally selected it while trying to find 'Hot Potato'). When combined with social media and website numbers, yet again, one of my wild musical adventures had been viewed by more than a million people. And that didn't include the hundreds of thousands of *Sunrise* viewers who watched the video clip premiere live, in its entirety, in our prime-time slot of 8 a.m. Madness.

I hosted the 'world premiere' of my song with some of my new target demographic at Little Zac's Day Care in Sydney. Thankfully, the feedback was mainly positive – but, of course, a true performer only remembers the negatives.

A few of the children were brutally honest in their feedback. One of them said, 'Umm, it's a bit cringe.' I responded by saying, 'Yeah, so are most of my segments.'

The next kid was about five years old and he said, 'It's too babyish.' Ouch.

A savage little girl then looked me dead in the eyes and said, 'It's one of those songs that's not very good, but it still gets stuck in your head.' The ultimate backhanded compliment.

We were inundated with photos and videos from mums, dads and their babies and toddlers reacting to the song. It was such a thrill seeing them doing the dance and singing along in their lounge rooms. A friend sent me a very funny post from a lady who was obviously confused by the whole situation and wrote, 'I just turned on Channel Seven to watch the news and this is on? What the f**k is happening?' Beneath that completely valid question was a vision of me dancing around as a cat and seductively stroking my whiskers. You're welcs.

As The Wiggles concert drew closer, Sean and I decided I should perform the song live and in front of a crowd to ensure I was match fit. We put the call out on *Sunrise* for schools to apply to host my debut live performance of 'Half Man, Half Cat'. More than a hundred schools from right around the country applied within a couple of hours. The eventual winner was Templestowe Valley Primary School, a performing arts school in Melbourne. One of the teachers, Miss McCormack, followed me on Instagram, so she was right across the entire arc and knew exactly what we were looking for. In her pitch she dressed the students in cats' ears, created colourful signs and even shared a snippet of some kids doing dance choreography to the song. *I* didn't know the dance choreography yet. And it was my song!

Sean always gets to the location earlier than I do. Some mornings he'll message me before I arrive with something like, 'You're going to enjoy this one,' and he'll often give me a little heads up on what to expect or look out for.

On the morning of our visit to Templestowe Valley he wrote, 'You're not going to believe this school – it's like the whole thing was built for you. Brace yourself.'

He was right. On arrival, I was greeted by around four hundred very enthusiastic students. Ninety per cent of them were dressed up as cats. They had little tails, stick-on whiskers, pointy cat ears – there was nothing understated about it. Some of them were dressed in cat suits, some had their faces painted, others were wearing cat T-shirts. So many different types of cats: leopards, moggies, Garfield, lions, tigers, Cat in the Hat – they all had their own interpretation. It was certainly a vibe.

An enormous sign hung from the gym wall, and it said, 'Welcome Sam Mac & #HalfManHalfCat'. They even used our official hashtag and correct branding. Swoon.

Sean was right: they were my people.

Miss McCormack wore a dress with a picture of my cat Coco on it. The principal was even wearing a cat onesie. Tremendous commitment.

Off the air we worked the kids very hard. There's a call-and-response part in the song – 'When I say "Cat", you say "Meow"' – and it might sound simple, but it only works if the timing is sharp. We ran through this part whenever we had downtime throughout the morning. We had the kids rehearse it at least twenty times. It had to be bang on. Do you think Lady Gaga just rocked up for her Super Bowl halftime show with no rehearsals? Absolutely not. And, yes, I did just compare my performance at a primary school to Lady Gaga's iconic concert in front of 117 million viewers. Come to think of it, my costume was probably more inappropriate than Gaga's. Particularly around children.

The time for the segment arrived and it played out to perfection. We'd worked them into a frenzy and even the viewers at home could feel how electric the atmosphere was in that school gym. The kids were dancing and meowing and waving their paws in the air like they just didn't care.

I said on air, 'This is like Coachella for six-year-olds.'

It made me extremely happy. You couldn't help but smile or laugh. Even the head of News and Current Affairs, Craig McPherson, texted Sean and me saying, 'Brilliant job'. That meant a lot. Getting a text like that from Craig is about as rare as me demonstrating any actual knowledge of the weather. Rare, but welcomed.

And then the big finale: 19 November 2019. That was the day I became a Wiggle.

I'm sitting in the dressing room watching a dancer carefully apply my whiskers. Hanging up behind me are the four iconic skivvies. In pristine condition and ready to wiggle. It's getting real now.

Suddenly a familiar face enters my dressing room. It's Jeff! Jeff of 'Wake up, Jeff' fame. Another OG Wiggle! We had a brief chat. He was such a friendly guy, although I'm sure he was sent in as an intimidation tactic to remind me not to screw this up and ruin The Wiggles franchise forever. Thanks, Jeff.

The curtains are drawn and The Wiggles drive on stage in the big red car. I can barely hear 'Toot Toot, Chugga

Chugga, Big Red Car' playing through the speakers over the deafening screams of five thousand rabid young fans. Madness!

I'm side of stage, watching the show. Loving the show. Almost forgetting that I'm about to be IN THE SHOW! I'm used to doing some pretty out-there things in this job, so it takes a lot to really stop me in my tracks. But I vividly remember watching all of the colours moving around in slow motion on stage and thinking to myself, *Holy shit, I'm about to be a bloody Wiggle*. I was nervous. Mainly about remembering the lyrics and doing a good job. I wanted to repay the faith Anthony and The Wiggles had shown in me by allowing me to join this ride.

The stage manager shows me to my position and tells me to follow the green arrow and enter at the end of the ballerina song. It's dark and there are curtains everywhere. The ballerina song ends. I ready myself then head towards the stage. I'm about to open the curtain when *thud* – I am hit in the face by something coming off stage via the same curtain. It is Dorothy the Dinosaur and she's bloody huge. I bet this wouldn't happen to Lady Gaga.

I pull myself together and go for it, slightly dazed.

Simon the Red Wiggle introduces me: 'Everyone, we'd like you to give a big cheer for a special friend of ours. It's Sam Mac with "Half Man, Half Cat".'

The song begins, 'Growing up as a young boy, I was trying to find my place, I took a look in the mirror, I found whiskers on my face.' Before I know it, the song is done. And I haven't screwed it up!

The crowd's response is louder than I expected. A solid, semi-believable cheer. Although I can't help but think they are cheering the fact that my song being finished means they are now closer to seeing more of Yellow Wiggle Emma.

I am about to exit the stage but Anthony has other ideas. There's a theme here. Anthony asks the crowd if they'd like to see a dog versus cat dance-off. Now this I am not prepared for. And obviously inside the Wags the Dog costume is a very young and fit professional dancer.

Of course I give it my all (yes, and). But I never stood a chance. It was like setting a dance-off between Justin Timberlake and Clive Palmer. Thanks, Anto! Needless to say I lose the dance-off and my big moment is completely upstaged by Wags the Dog.

The Wiggles experience fills my soul with joy every time I think or talk about it. It combined many of my true loves: music, creativity, risk-taking, absurdity and, of course, cats. Even now, more than a year on, I still regularly receive videos of kids singing or dancing to the song. I believe it's known in the biz as a 'certified banger'.

I also have a handful of friends who will never forgive me. They speak of the regular tantrums their toddler has until they cave and put on 'the cat song'. Purrfect. I've never been prouder.

14

2020

I decided to write a chapter about the year 2020 as I figured it would be a form of cheap therapy.

I'm sure everybody reading this could write their own chapter, or book, on the unmitigated disaster that was 2020. You know it's been a shocker of a year when the year itself becomes an adjective – i.e. 'Oh man, my bike got stolen, that's so 2020.'

Collectively, we survived a babushka doll of trauma. The year started with one of the worst bushfire seasons in our nation's history. Somehow, we rallied together and got through it. As the bushfires finally ended, almost to the day, we were hit by COVID-19, a once-in-a-lifetime global pandemic. And just when we thought things couldn't get any worse – and it still pains me to say this – the Adelaide Crows got the wooden spoon.

The 2019–20 Australian bushfire season, known as Black Summer, burnt over 17 million hectares, destroyed 3094 homes, and tragically killed at least 33 people. The Australian Academy of Science also estimated that more than 1 billion animals were killed. It's truly horrific, and so devastatingly unfair.

A theme of this book has been how little I talk about the weather. But for the first few months of 2020 it was ALL I was talking about. Like most Australians, I desperately wanted to do my bit. I didn't exactly know what 'my bit' was, but I couldn't sit still and do nothing.

I edited videos encouraging people to donate. One of my videos, set to the Powderfinger song 'The Day You Come', received hundreds of thousands of views, and I even had people from overseas telling me it prompted them to donate. It wasn't much, but it was something.

Another way I contributed was by visiting the Port Macquarie Koala Hospital. I shared stories on *Sunrise*, on my social media, and did radio interviews with anyone who'd listen. As a big animal lover, I'm still haunted by the footage of those helpless creatures being overcome by the fires. Heartbreaking.

As the fires were winding down I set off on a 'Road to Recovery' tour with *Sunrise*. I visited five of the regions most severely affected by the fires. It was a big, draining week. But so worth it. The warm welcome those communities gave me when they were at their lowest point holds a very special place in my heart. I want to acknowledge the beautiful people of Kangaroo Island, Lakes Entrance, Eden, Narooma and Batemans Bay.

The team at Channel Seven asked me to write an article about my experiences on that trip. I remember sitting on the deck of my accommodation in Batemans Bay with my laptop and a beer, wondering what I should write.

The first thing that came to mind was the smell. Only days earlier I'd stood among the charcoal stumps that used to be trees. I'd never encountered such a potent, lingering burning smell. It was confronting. And I couldn't take my mind off the fact that these trees used to be homes. Homes for our precious wildlife. It made me quite emotional. Again, I had flashbacks to the news footage of koalas desperately crawling onto the road away from the unbearable heat.

The more I thought about the article, the more I thought about the people I'd met. The communities. The Australian spirit. It sounds clichéd but it's true. Mateship and looking out for one another are still integral parts of our country's DNA. I hope we never lose that.

The article started to emerge as a poem. I wanted to find the positives in a dire situation, and the positives were predominantly in the shape of everyday Australians. Here is the poem I wrote at the end of that trip, titled 'Australia Stood Up':

The heart of our country was ripped from our chest
Australia on fire, the ultimate test
We've copped them before, but this wasn't the same
Our pubs, schools and houses, all up in flames

Good people were lost, they'll never return
and no child should see our animals burn
Australia on fire, all over the news
Respect to our firies, the world's greatest crews

As the smoke slowly fades, and the green reappears
we meet unsung heroes, who'll bring you to tears
They're not in it for glory, not in it for fame
They help coz it's right, and you'd do the same

It's Steve with his tugboat, on the water in Eden
letting strangers stay the night, and offering to feed 'em
He kept the elderly safe, when they didn't know what to do
and the pet cats and dogs, yeah, he let them stay too

It's the big burly truckies on Kangaroo Island
cradling koalas like babies, and staying beside 'em
And two bucks from every coffee sold at the cafe by Jan
is gonna help build new clubrooms, for the Saints and
   their fans

Anita at Lakes Entrance, her home is gone
but she greets me with a smile and says, 'Well, life
   goes on'
It's the kids giving toys to the families in need
coz you're never too young to do a good deed

Our heart was on fire, and we'll never be the same
But that heart is still beating, and soon there'll be rain
Australia stood up, our voices were loud
Australia stood up, and that makes me proud.

And then, with Australia still reeling from the bushfires, we were punched violently in the face by a global pandemic.

If I'd watched a Hollywood blockbuster pre-COVID-19 where the plot was that the whole world has to wear masks, not touch each other, ideally not go to work, and essentially be prisoners in their own homes, all because some guy allegedly ate a bat at a market in China, I would've stopped the movie in the first ten minutes because it was too far-fetched. But, alas, this was our reality in 2020.

And who did we turn to with Doomsday upon us? Joe Exotic, of course. Like a lot of people, I barely noticed the pandemic in the first month as I was in self-imposed isolation bingeing *Tiger King* on Netflix. But all good things must come to an end. Something Carole Baskin said to her first husband. Allegedly.

When you boil things down, my role is really about two things: travel and people. COVID-19 meant that both of those things were ripped away, almost overnight. We had to adjust. Or – and apologies in advance for using one of the most overused words of 2020 – we had to pivot.

The Human Emoji and I very quickly knew what we needed to do. We had to turn our segments into a space for good vibes only. We needed to inject some positivity into a very scary, uncertain time. Kids watch our show. We don't want kids thinking the world is all doom and gloom. And even adults need a little breather from the loop of negativity in the news cycle.

I was chatting to my great mate Sarah Connell. She told me about her sister Jacinta and how Jacinta's small business was really struggling due to COVID-19. Jacinta had a few staff who relied on that work, and she was doing everything she could, desperately trying to keep the business going.

I got off the phone and it hit me: there must be thousands and thousands of wonderful small businesses in exactly the same boat. I had an idea.

I spoke to The Human Emoji and our executive producer, Michael Pell, and the concept of 'Plugapalooza' was born. A mini festival promoting small businesses of Australia.

I set the target of promoting one hundred small businesses in three days. I posted about it on my social media that night, and less than twelve hours after having the idea it was on air to the nation. That's one thing I love about my job. The immediacy. And the access to a platform that reaches such a large audience.

I started the show with a plug for Jacinta's Brightside Deli in Adelaide, because it was her story that inspired the concept.

We were all blown away by the volume and diversity of small businesses reaching out. We were inundated. The Human Emoji had stopped by Officeworks for a whiteboard that enabled us to tick off a small business every time we plugged one. It wasn't the slickest-looking operation, but it was positive and the audience could feel that our hearts were in the right place. A little twenty-second plug on TV might not seem like much, but big businesses pay tens of thousands of dollars for those spots. So for these small businesses to get that moment in the limelight, it was a pretty big deal. It was making a difference. And, probably more importantly, it was lifting their spirits and giving them some hope.

My challenge was to make the spots entertaining. I didn't want to do three days of just reading out small business names. It had to be interesting. So we really pushed ourselves creatively. For one of the plugs I grabbed a yoga mat and delivered a script I'd written, while doing the downward dog:

'Hi, I'm television icon Sam Mac. My job can be very stressful, and I've been known to get severe tension in my shoulders. From carrying the show. But not anymore, thanks to Western Wellness Yoga Studio in Point Cook. It's a scary time, Australia, but I'm here to remind you to take a breath, do some yoga, and *namaste*-positive.'

It was the kind of TV I'd seen growing up, on highlight reels of Bert Newton and Graham Kennedy. It was exhilarating. And it was coming from a good place, so we couldn't lose.

By day two of Plugapalooza we'd received over three thousand submissions from small businesses. An incredible response, and an insight for us into just how much the idea had resonated. But it also highlighted the desperation of many of those businesses, and the urgent need to do something to help. It was bittersweet knowing that we were only going to be able to plug one hundred of them.

As I've mentioned earlier, I try my best to at least read and acknowledge every single message people send me. Naturally, some stand out more than others. I have such a clear recollection of receiving this note from a lady named Kate Inglish. The moment I read it, I screenshotted it, because I knew we had to help her:

> Hi Sam, my name is Kate. I own a baby clothing boutique called Kate Inglish Designs. We're a tiny shop in Nowra, on the NSW coast. We've had a rough trot this year as our region was also hit by the fires in January. I'm only months away from reaching our ten year anniversary. But I'm terrified I'm not going to make it. I've put my heart and soul into this place and my beautiful customers who mean the world to me. I've already gone into my buffer from Christmas and I'm scared because I don't have my buffer anymore. Even when things are good, I only just get by. I'm sure there's businesses more deserving than mine, but I thought I'd write just in case. Thank you for your segments and for thinking of small businesses.

The fact that even when Kate was clearly struggling she was still thinking of other people more deserving just made me want to help her even more.

I texted Larry Emdur. Yeah, I've got his number. No biggie. Stop bringing it up.

I asked Larry to record a few lines in a fun little advert for Kate's business. Larry was more than happy to help out. So the next morning live on air I shared Kate's letter then played an official endorsement from TV's Larry Emdur:

'Hi, I'm Larry Emdur. When I think about self-isolating, I think about making babies.' [Marvin Gaye music starts playing]

'Come on down to Kate Inglish Designs in Nowra for all your baby needs. I know I will. Hey, Sylvie, do you want to self-isolate again?'

The team in the studio had a good laugh. And I made a point of saying how valuable it was to have Larry Emdur endorsing Kate's business: 'Do you know how much Larry could've charged for that? He could've bought another Bondi property!'

Minutes after the segment had aired, I checked my phone and Kate had posted a video. She was in tears. I could feel how much that meant to her in such a challenging time. It's moments like that where I know I'm doing exactly what I should be doing. These moments are bigger than television, they're real-life connections. And I treasure them. They put fuel in my tank for when the job gets tough.

Kate messaged me later that week and it was extremely humbling:

> You have no idea how much this has impacted my business. My website crashed when the segment aired. It's never had that volume of traffic. So many people have been calling to place their orders. The phone hasn't stopped all day. I even had people dropping into the store to make purchases and to tell me they saw me on *Sunrise*. I've had more orders in 3 days than I'd normally get in 3 months. I honestly can't thank you, Larry and the team enough. I've got a buffer now. You've saved my business.

Commercial TV cops a bad rap sometimes, and rightly so. But it still has the power to genuinely make a difference. And I'm extremely proud of moments like this.

I eventually met Kate when we were on a road trip along the coast. I dropped into her shop unannounced and gave her a big hug. Such a lovely, genuine woman who got the support she deserved in her time of need. If you're ever in Nowra, drop in and make a purchase. Tell them Larry sent you.

I often look back and wonder what on earth we did with our segments for half the year with no travel and no people. How did we fill all of that air time? It certainly wasn't with detailed weather analysis. It definitely challenged us creatively, but we just kept going. And I think the true creatives shone through during COVID-19 on TV and online.

Our technical team, with Paul Matulin at the helm, became gurus of using Zoom for live TV. We were all adjusting and learning on the fly. I hosted kids from around the country in a virtual classroom with 'Mr Mac'. I dedicated mornings to our 'Healthcare Heroes' and our 'Learning Legends'. Recognising the outstanding work and personal sacrifice from our medical staff and teachers. Plugapalooza made a comeback and we promoted even more small businesses in need. We did a 'Virtual A–Z', checking in via Zoom on towns around Australia. That feature alone provided us with twenty-six days of content.

I even created my own quiz, 'Sam Mac's Virtual Pub Quiz'. We had a different contestant from each state via Zoom and I could never have predicted how wild it would get. It almost became a show within a show. We had our own graphics at the start of each segment, we had promotional merchandise, we had a golden schooner trophy, and every champion of Sam Mac's Virtual Pub Quiz received a bottle of wine shaped like a kangaroo. Contestants poured green milk all over their bodies, danced with novelty-size bear heads, gyrated in bikinis, tweaked their nipples while eating FruChocs, and we even had one guy jump into Lake Burley Griffin live on air. Mayhem. And we got away with it because everyone had gone a little nuts during lockdown. Perfecto.

The complicated part was around mid-year in 2020. We were starting to return to some form of normality. Of course, precautions were still in place, and we weren't completely out of the woods, but there was some light at the end of the tunnel. Unless you were living in Victoria.

Many of my closest friends and family live in Victoria. My manager, the dynamic Melissa Harvey, is in Victoria. Ordinarily I travel there every month for something, and I know the place and its people very well. I was chatting to Victorians everyday in some capacity, so I had a real sense of how much the extended, and seemingly never-ending, lockdown was affecting them. They had the strictest conditions in the world at one point. And they were only a one-hour flight away from me. I had mates who were normally fun and upbeat people sounding genuinely lost. I could hear it in their voices. It was like they were living in a different country, and they'd done nothing wrong.

Again, The Human Emoji and I wanted to contribute some positivity to the situation. So we pitched a very simple concept: 'Showing love to Victoria'. We dedicated a week of our crosses to lifting Victorians' spirits in lockdown.

We promoted small businesses, put loved ones in touch live on air, we had comedians and musicians performing on the show, we even had singalongs with the seniors of Victoria, many of them using Zoom for the first time in their lives.

Dr Chris Brown and I also decided, over a few drinks on a Saturday night, to perform song requests on Instagram for Victorians in lockdown. We had an unbelievable response. Sure, they were stuck at home with nowhere to go, but we interpreted their response as genuine passion for our obvious musical talent. The great thing about doing these requests at Chris's house is that he has a props department more elaborate than most major Hollywood film sets.

Our videos very quickly became more about the visuals. At one point Chris casually revealed that he had not one but three crayfish costumes. Three! On this particular night our pal, Thirsty Merc front man Rai Thistlethwayte, was over. So we grabbed the costumes and belted out a song. It only occurred to me the next day that I'd missed an opportunity for one of the great puns of our time. As soon as he put that suit on Rai should've been referred to as 'Cray Fishlethwayte'. I'm still disappointed in myself for missing that one. But hey, at least it made the book.

It was around this time that Chris and I decided to form a band. Just when you thought 2020 couldn't get any worse.

And, yes, it's the biggest red flag that we're both nearing a midlife crisis.

The band was named in an online competition by my *Sunrise* compadre Edwina Bartholomew. Introducing ... Tone Deaf Leopard.

Upon formation, we had already made history as the first band ever featuring a qualified vet and an unqualified weatherman. Almost immediately, Chris and I knew who we were. At Tone Deaf Leopard, we always say, the music comes fourth. Well behind elaborate costumes, choreography and professional lighting.

On 8 November 2020 at approximately 1 a.m., Tone Deaf Leopard played our highly unanticipated first live gig at the Bronte Beach rotunda in Sydney. Due to COVID-19 restrictions (and a complete lack of interest), the official attendance was zero. The set included one song, 'Live at the Rotunda', and lasted just twenty-three seconds. We then conducted a two-hour photo shoot, again staying true to our motto, 'It's music for your eyes'. I'm really proud of what Chris and I are doing with TDL, and we've even been described (by ourselves) as 'the breakout stars of this pandemic'.

Like a lot of parents and grandparents around the country, Loretta was focused on one major question throughout the pandemic: 'Will we be able to see you for Christmas?' Every year I find a way to get home to Adelaide for Christmas with the family. But for a while in the curious beast that was 2020, it wasn't looking likely.

Thankfully, in October, we finally had approval for a work trip to Adelaide. I decided to keep it a secret from everyone, including Mum and Dad. My sister Paula was in on it and we arranged for the family to be over at her place for dinner.

One of my favourite things about Loretta is that she's extremely easy to surprise (see earlier story on André Rieu). Loretta is so pure and takes everyone's word as the truth. That's why it's so much fun to betray her trust.

=2

I called Mum on that Sunday evening. Within the first twenty seconds of the call she said, 'So, will you be able to get back to Adelaide for Christmas, Sam?' Game on. I don't know why I get such a thrill out of blatantly lying to my darling mother.

'Unfortunately it's not looking likely, Mum,' I said. 'Channel Seven are being so strict about travel. Even Kochie said he doesn't want us travelling and you know what he's like when he gets his mind set on something, he's like Kim Jong-un.'

Little did Loretta know but as I was saying all of this I was actually out the front of Paula's house, walking through the door, about to see her in the flesh. Obviously I was filming the whole thing, because a wise man once said 'content never sleeps'. (It was me. I was that wise man.)

By this point I was really having fun with it.

'What's the weather like today in Adelaide?' I asked Mum.

Loretta went on to give me a weather report more detailed than the ones I give on *Sunrise*. Which wasn't hard.

Next, everybody started laughing. They couldn't keep up the facade any longer. Loretta looked up and saw me holding the phone, standing two metres away from her. Gotcha!

I hadn't seen Mum and Dad in eight months. The longest I've ever gone in my life without seeing them. Those hugs were extra special. And even in the midst of this surprise reunion, Loretta remained on point: 'But will you still be coming home for Christmas?'

The Adelaide visit was part of a last-minute work trip sprung on me by the bosses, who really wanted me in Queensland. Due to Queensland's extreme border restrictions, I needed to spend fourteen days out of Sydney to be able to enter the state. After ten days in Adelaide and four days in Canberra I was granted entry.

The AFL grand final and a number of other events, combined with the fact I couldn't travel home on weekends, meant this would be the longest work trip I'd ever done. Six weeks on the road. Thankfully my old housemate Ally, who some of you might know as 'The Australian Princess' circa 2005 (she still regularly wears the tiara), was kind enough to look after the cats while I was away.

This meant that after forty-two days apart, I was primed for another emotional reunion with my beloved rescue cats. While I was away I visualised the moment where I'd get to hug the girls so many times.

Obviously I was filming my approach to Ally's house (content never sleeps) and as I opened the door I saw Coco sitting on the couch.

'Coco! Daddy's home! Did you miss me?' I said in a pitch reminiscent of a fourteen-year-old girl.

Not only was Coco's Resting Bitch Face fully activated but she savagely turned her head away as soon as I walked through the door.

I tried to give her a hug, but she could not have been less interested.

And Catra ... well, she was under the couch and didn't emerge for almost an hour. It was like they'd completely forgotten I existed.

Pure indifference. It's part of why I love cats. They're like the outrageously hot girl: they don't have to do any work and you'll still desperately seek their affection. And isn't it crazy that even with a former Australian Princess in the house, Coco was still the biggest diva.

Another milestone moment in 2020 was the opening of the Queensland borders to New South Wales and Victoria. Queensland premier Annastacia Palaszczuk took a very cautious approach to borders, and it was a major news event when Queensland finally welcomed interstate travellers on 30 November.

Of course, our producers wanted me there to cover the arrival of that very first flight. But being there wasn't as easy as it sounds. We're a breakfast TV show, starting at 5.30 a.m. The first flight was scheduled to arrive at

7.30 a.m. If I'd flown to Brisbane the night before, I'd still be expected to quarantine for two weeks. That was not an option. Thankfully, Brisbane Airport also really wanted us there, so they very generously arranged a charter flight. The Queensland border was officially opening at 1 a.m., so our charter flight departing Sydney at 2 a.m. would enable us to smoothly enter Queensland without having to quarantine.

At 2 a.m. I got on a regular-sized Qantas flight with The Human Emoji, cameraman Tim Stewart and link technician Trevor Bowdidge. We had the entire flight to ourselves, along with the crew (and a pilot, obviously). It was quite surreal looking around at an empty plane. And I still wasn't in business class.

When we landed in Brisbane I headed straight to the airport hotel for one hour of sleep. Literally. Then back to the airport ready for the show.

As we approached 7.30 a.m. the crowds were building. We were now dealing with what was essentially a media scrum. Radio shows, photographers, online journalists and, of course, the other TV networks.

When the first flight finally arrived it was like a gaggle of seagulls fighting over a hot chip. Everybody wanted that Hollywood moment of loved ones being reunited. Unfortunately, and rather hilariously, the majority of passengers getting off the flight were just there for work.

'Is this a special day for you?' I asked. 'Nah, just going to work, mate,' the passenger responded.

It was so ridiculous, it became funny. And it got worse.

'This is an exciting day, isn't it?' I said to one lady as she walked through the gate.

'Well, I'm actually here for my aunty's funeral,' she responded.

Of course, I could never have predicted that, and the reality of live TV is that anything can happen.

Finally, we found the moment we were hoping for: a young dad embracing his wife and daughter after six months apart. It was like a real-life scene from *Love Actually*. There were hugs, kisses and tears. I tried to ask how they were feeling, but understandably they were too caught up in the moment. So I had to ad lib: 'Nothing like a precious moment shared between your family, fourteen camera crews and a random weather guy.'

By this stage the cross had been going for about six minutes. Almost twice the length of my regular crosses. Michael Pell was in my ear, saying, 'Keep going, this is great, keep going.' So I just kept chatting to any passenger within arm's-length.

Randomly, TV's Mike Goldman appeared.

'I wasn't on the flight,' he said, 'I just grabbed a bag and walked over here to get on TV.'

By this stage it was getting very loose. That's my favourite type of TV. I noticed the Channel Nine reporter jumping in front of me to get to some of the passengers, so I made a call on the fly to incorporate that in my cross.

'I'm not sure who this lady is, I don't know her name, but I feel like she's trying to cut my lunch,' I said.

From there, I made what would turn out to be a rather controversial decision. I decided to put myself on Channel Nine's *Today* show.

It's an unspoken rule that in a situation like that you stay out of each other's shots, and particularly those of your rival breakfast show. But these were extraordinary circumstances and, in my defence, they started it. I was merely retaliating, admittedly in a completely over-the-top manner, but I thought we could have some fun with the ridiculousness of the situation.

At one point I grabbed the *Today* show microphone and said, 'Welcome back to the *Today* show.'

I later found out that Channel Nine cut away from the live cross as soon as that happened. It was absolute chaos. The segment had reached the eight-minute mark and it ended with me lying on the floor.

'I think I just interviewed one hundred and thirty seven passengers. I need a lie-down,' I said.

In the next cross I approached the *Today* reporter who was lingering near the bins. I'll happily put my hand up and say I was quite delirious by this point. One hour of sleep, remember.

I thought I'd extend the olive branch. I introduced myself and asked her name. She had a bit of a laugh and said, 'Are we on air?' I told her we were on air and said, 'I just wanted to apologise for getting in your shot, but you were in ours a few times first so it was just a little payback.'

She then tried to highlight the fact that I wasn't Queensland-based by saying, 'Welcome to Queensland, Sam,' with a sprinkling of sass.

I enjoyed it and said, 'Thank you, it's great to be here.'

She then said, 'Let the games begin,' with even more sass.

Again, I was on board with that and said, rather provocatively, 'Ooh, I love games.'

Next, she held up her mic and said, 'Ahh, are we doing a live cross?' to which I replied, 'Yes, but your mic's not plugged in, so I win.'

Okay, that was definitely my sleep deprivation kicking in. But it was all in good fun.

Off air, I finally got her name, which was Aislin Kriukelis, and she was lovely! I gave her some chocolates, thanked her for being a good sport and we even posed for a few *Anchorman*-style photos.

I could never have predicted how big a response that morning's segment would receive. I checked my phone and saw hundreds of Instagram notifications, tags and text messages. It had certainly made an impact.

I think people were fascinated by the forbidden nature of appearing on or mentioning the rival show. The Human Emoji and I both looked at each other with the same confused expression. We knew there were some great moments, but it was so long and chaotic we didn't really know how it would be perceived.

The news websites had a field day. The first headline I saw was on the *Daily Mail*: 'Channel Nine is "furious" after *Sunrise* weatherman Sam Mac broke protocol by "ambushing" *Today*'s live broadcast from Brisbane Airport.'

The thing I found fascinating about this was the use of the term 'protocol'. I was not aware of any protocol. Perhaps I missed protocol training day? I shared the article on my socials with the admittedly antagonistic hashtag of #ProtoLOL.

News.com.au described me as 'the face of car crash TV'. I kind of liked that one, and may use it as a new email signature.

We went there to cover a story, and somehow we became the story.

The clash even made it onto *Media Watch* on the ABC. Something I definitely wear as a badge of honour.

The feedback and reactions gained some serious momentum, and continued to snowball throughout the day. Thankfully they were 90 per cent positive, but some people were genuinely angry about it. I think I would handle it exactly the same way if I were in those circumstances again. It's live TV, you have to go with your gut, and that's exactly what I did. Aislin approached it from a journalistic perspective, and I approached it from an entertainment or comedic perspective. No one did anything wrong.

And, ultimately, it's just TV. Some people need to lighten up a little and remember how to smile. I can now proudly say that 'I wake up with (and occasionally on) *Today*'.

Later that night, as I was reading through the messages and processing what had happened, I received a text from Dad:

Hi son, great work this morning. You were under incredible pressure. Your ad-lib talent was really tested, but you rose to the challenge. Mum and I are so proud.

And that was the only opinion that really mattered. Well, that and the opinion of my boss, who didn't fire me.

•

I find myself now in the precarious position of attempting to (M)accurately summarise and complete this chapter about the year 2020. Strangely, there's one story that comes to mind. And I think you'll agree it's as 2020 as you can get.

It started out innocently enough. I was at a doggy day care centre in the Sydney suburb of Zetland. In our 6 a.m. cross I was chatting to the lovely husband and wife who owned the business.

In the opening twenty seconds of the segment I could hear the studio hosts laughing. A lot of people don't realise that I can't see the studio hosts when I'm on location, I can only hear them. So as I was interviewing the couple I was trying to figure out what the hosts were laughing at. Then Kochie told me to turn around.

Directly behind me were two dogs who were ... well, what's the polite way to say this? ROOTING!

A black dog had mounted a brown dog and Australia was getting a visual demonstration of why the position is colloquially called 'doggie style'. It's a lot to deal with as you're munching on your Weet-Bix.

We hastily separated the two dogs and attempted to continue with the interview like it was no big deal. Barely ten seconds had passed and I heard the hosts laughing again. Sure enough, I turned around and it was round two. This time with added gusto. Now we had to embrace it.

'We've had more action in this segment than we had on *Farmer Wants a Wife*,' I said. The studio hosts were now doubled over in tears of laughter. I thought it would be a good time to throw to the weather for a little breather.

During the weather the doggy day care owners moved the black dog into another section. A forced walk of shame.

We returned after the weather and recommenced our interview about the wonderful facilities at doggy day care. Then, ten seconds into part two, I heard the studio laughing again.

I turned around and this time saw a cocker spaniel ... well, what's the polite way to say this? TAKING A DUMP!

A live review of my segment, perhaps?

Often, the most memorable moments of live TV are when things go wrong. I live for those moments. But even I was in utter shock at how this was playing out on air. We'd been in the centre for an hour before this cross and it had been extremely uneventful.

Of course, the hosts were covering their eyes and struggling to breathe with laughter as three perfect nuggets of cocker spaniel business were dropped along the floor.

Before the owners even had a chance to clean up the mess, another dog appeared from nowhere, probably from a grassy knoll, and proceeded to EAT THE POO. Truly unbelievable scenes! And the perfect ending to this four-part comedy sequence. If it wasn't so disgusting I'd describe it as 'chef's kiss' content. You simply cannot plan or prepare for moments like this.

Within one hour of the incident the *Daily Mail* headline read: '*Sunrise* weatherman Sam Mac is left mortified during a segment about dog day care as two pooches start HUMPING each other on camera.' Below the headline was a split screen photo of two dogs going for it, and my face. Hmm, maybe I really am the face of car crash TV.

That incident at doggy day care was a stunning metaphor for 2020. We entered with the truest of intentions but then, through no fault of our own, it all went to shit.

Epilogue

You made it to the end of the book! I made it to the end of the book! We made it to the end of the book!

I'm officially an author. Which means I'll be growing a beard and wearing a monocle. I'll also be loudly and obnoxiously starting all of my anecdotes at parties with, 'Well, as an *author* ...'

But seriously, I don't think I have the words to express how much it means to me that you gave me your eyes, ears, mind and, hopefully, heart for the past 292 pages. It astounds me that you even bought this book. You paid money to read my story! (Unless it was an unwanted gift and you had to do your best impression of Loretta receiving an André Rieu CD.)

Writing this book has been one of the most challenging projects I've ever undertaken. But it's also been one of the most rewarding. My mindset is always so focused on what's next, but this book has forced me to look back and reflect. It's also forced me to look analytically at who I am, and why I do what I do. And thankfully, I'm proud of what I've discovered.

I don't get it right every time. In fact, I often get it wrong. But I keep getting up, showing up and having a crack. The themes that I hope shine through in my work, and in this book, come from a place of authenticity. I love people, and I enjoy being silly and using creativity to make strangers smile, but I'm also searching for something more meaningful. A deeper connection. Mental health, animal rescue, and shining a light on good humans – they are my pillars. That won't change.

I don't consider this book a finished product. Even though it's written, and published, it's not final to me. It's merely a beginning. I'm now standing by for your feedback, questions and experiences. I see this book as a conversation starter. And I genuinely welcome you to contact me on Instagram (sammacinsta), Facebook or Twitter (mrsammac), or at the following address: <u>accidentalweatherman@hotmail.com</u>

This might be an odd note to end on, but I've never really had the platform to say this: Please say hello to me in public, and please never apologise for it. On countless occasions I've received direct messages from people saying, 'I saw you at the food court but I didn't want to bother you' or 'We were sitting behind you on a flight but you were listening to music'. Just say hello! The other thing that baffles me is how apologetic people are for 'interrupting' or asking for a selfie. This is me, putting it on the record: I LOVE meeting you guys. I really do. Some of my favourite interactions and ongoing connections have grown from someone simply saying hello. And I love a good selfie. In fact, I'll even treat you to a quick #Saminar on how to get the most out of lighting and angles.

So, someday, sometime, somewhere I look forward to meeting you in person and catching up for a chat. But please, whatever you do, don't ask me about the weather.

Macknowledgements

Loretta, your unwavering love and support has shaped me into the man I am today. Your kindness, empathy and morals are with me every step of the way, no matter where I am. You're constantly telling me (and the poor, unsuspecting customers at Tip Top Dry Cleaners in Adelaide) that you're proud to call me your son. Well, I want you to know that I'm even prouder to call you my mum.

Sam senior, this job has challenged me on a daily basis to create instant connections with strangers, and to make it entertaining. It's only in the past few years I've realised that being your son has been a lifetime of training for this very role. You make people feel special, you're happy to be the butt of a joke, you're clever but down-to-earth, and you have the innate gift of always being able to miraculously locate a guitar – whether the audience want it or not. But above all, you have a slightly inflated belief in your own ability (particularly on the soccer field). Oh, did I mention I've represented Australia at international schoolboy level soccer? Thank you, Dad, for leading me to the fulfilment of some of my wildest dreams. And thank you for accepting that you'll only ever be the second most entertaining Samuel in this family.

Paula, even though we don't see each other as much as we'd like to, I think you know that your sense of humour, love for animals, straight-talking, no-nonsense attitude and obsession with karaoke is with me everywhere I go. You, Dave, Ella and Bailey support me with such fierce loyalty that I know I'm never really alone. And, after everything you've done for me, it's my absolute pleasure to give you a 10 per cent discount on the purchase of your copy of this book.

Human Emoji, you already got an entire chapter. Don't be greedy.

Kochie, you sent me an incredible text message of support on my first day filling in on *Sunrise*, before I even had the gig. You didn't have to do that and I'll never forget it. Sadly, our relationship has been all downhill since then, culminating in you inviting me as your corporate box guest for a Port Power finals game. It took all my might to pretend to be happy for you and your win that night. A rare form of torture for a Crows fan. I'm still recovering.

Samantha, you were my big sister on the show. We reached a point where we were so comfortable heckling one another that some audience members (and *Daily Mail* 'journalists') actually thought we hated each other. I wear that as a badge of honour. I loved discovering that you have a sense of humour as dark and twisted as mine. And I think that's a compliment, or a desperate cry for a few sessions with a psychiatrist. I was also privileged, off the air, to experience the caring, loyal side of you that not everybody gets to see. It means a lot. I can't wait to see what you do next, and thanks for teaching me to always take time to stop and smell the lavender.

Beretts, unquestionably one of the nicest blokes in television. Which is why it amuses me to joke about you having a sinister dungeon installed beneath your house. Obviously it's not true. Although I've never officially checked. I've learnt so much from you, mate, but mainly how to charge a higher rate for emcee gigs. Cheers.

Nat, I've watched firsthand as you've delivered live, breaking news under the most challenging circumstances. I don't think I've seen anyone do it better. You are unbelievably calm under the most intense pressure. But your ultimate gifts to me are your facial expressions during my more colourful segments. An RBF that even rivals Miss Coco's. An editor's dream.

Edwina, you broke down in tears live on air when I was officially announced as your replacement. You assured me it was because your family was there. Five years later and I'm still not convinced. Building a friendship with you has been one of the unexpected treats of this job, and I absolutely loved watching you get married (not in a creepy way, I was invited). And not that I'm trying to use my book as a platform to highlight inequality in media, but you were sent to a cotton farm on your first day of weather to interview people about cotton. I had to bungee jump. Just sayin. #Justice4MenInMedia

Michael Pell, the only executive producer I've ever met who looks like he's about to knock off from the control room at 9 a.m. to model on a Versace runway at 10 a.m. I'm lucky I didn't get you to edit this section or it would've turned into a glossy gallery of your perfectly lit promo shots. A rare glitch in the matrix has meant that you haven't aged since 2006. The curious case of Michael Pell. The J-Lo of Martin Place. I genuinely admire your leadership and willingness to take risks. You've backed me and created a space where I feel like anything is possible. I know you love memorable TV as much as I do and working with you is an exhilarating ride. You fight hard for your team and you're a winner. Please don't ever fire me.

Melissa Harvey, my manager of almost a decade! I connected with you instantly. You could see who I was and what I was capable of before many others. Right from the start, you, the inimitable Mark Klemens and the team at Profile were thinking big. It's contagious. Even during the quiet, uncertain times, you believed in me. You went in to bat for me. It's only now as I enjoy a rare moment of reflection that I realise you, we, have done many of those things we dreamt of a decade ago. I love that you are the person representing me. I have complete faith and trust in you on a personal and professional level. Thank you for guiding me through, Mel, and long may it continue. I don't think either of us have a choice. I haven't checked the contract, but I'm quite sure you're entitled to 20 per cent of my unborn child.

Sophie Hamley, publisher extraordinaire. Almost three years ago you slid into my DMs on Facebook asking me out to lunch. Initially I was taken aback by how forward women are in the age of social media, until I realised it was to discuss the possibility of working together on this very book. The time wasn't right back then, but our meeting planted the seed. It prompted me to take more notes, collect more stories. So when we revisited the idea in 2020, the time was right. People often say, 'I couldn't have done this without you.' Well, I could've done this without you, Sophie, but it wouldn't have been anywhere near as good, and it wouldn't have been released until 2028. You have a gift for storytelling. You helped me find my voice as a writer. And you have a memory that genuinely scares me. Thank you from the bottom of my heart for imagining this book before anyone else and then kicking my butt until it eventuated. This is your book too, weather you like it or not (that's another pun, pay it please). And a big thank you to Rebecca Allen, Bella Lloyd and the rest of the wonderful team at Hachette Australia.

Friends, if you've watched me on *Sunrise*, followed me on social media or just crossed paths with me on my travels, I consider you a friend. The job and the sacrifices that come with it can be relentless. There's definitely mornings where it's a hard slog. But the messages and comments and face-to-face meetings that I encounter with you guys always lift my spirits at exactly the right time. I'll never take that support for granted.

And finally, arguably the most important thank you of them all must go to the weather app on my iPhone. Without you, this just would not have been possible. Literally.